THE
GREEN
SMOOTHIE
GARDEN

THE
GREEN
SMOOTHIE
GARDEN

Grow Your Own Produce for the Most Nutritious Green Smoothie Recipes Possible!

Edited by Tracy Russell, founder of IncredibleSmoothies.com, and Catherine Abbott

Adams**media**

Avon, Massachusetts

Published by
Adams Media, a division of F+W Media, Inc.
57 Littlefield Street, Avon, MA 02322 U.S.A.
www.adamsmedia.com

Contains material adapted and abridged from *The Everything® Grow Your Own Vegetables Book*
by Catherine Abbott, copyright © 2010 by F+W Media, Inc., ISBN 10: 1-4405-0013-4, ISBN 13: 978-
1-4405-0013-8; *The Everything® Small-Space Gardening Book* by Catherine Abbott, copyright
© 2012 by F+W Media, Inc., ISBN 10: 1-4405-3060-2, ISBN 13: 978-1-4405-3060-9; and *The
Everything® Green Smoothies Book* by Britt Brandon with Lorena Novak Bull, RD, copyright ©
2011 by F+W Media, ISBN 10: 1-4405-2564-1, ISBN 13: 978-1-4405-2564-3.

ISBN 10: 1-4405-6837-5
ISBN 13: 978-1-4405-6837-4
eISBN 10: 1-4405-6838-3
eISBN 13: 978-1-4405-6838-1

Printed in the United States of America.

10 9 8 7 6 5 4 3 2 1

Library of Congress Cataloging-in-Publication Data

The green smoothie garden / edited by Tracy Russell and Catherine Abbott.
    p. cm.
  Includes bibliographical references and index.
  ISBN-13: 978-1-4405-6837-4 (pbk. : alk. paper)
  ISBN-10: 1-4405-6837-5 (pbk. : alk. paper)
  ISBN-13: 978-1-4405-6838-1 (eISBN)
  ISBN-10: 1-4405-6838-3 (eISBN)
  1. Vegetable gardening. 2. Herb gardening. 3. Smoothies (Beverages) I. Russell, Tracy.
II. Abbott, Catherine. III. Title: Grow your own produce for the most nutritious green smoothie
recipes possible.
  SB321.G8164 2013
  635--dc23
                    2013031082

Always follow safety and common-sense cooking protocol while using kitchen utensils, operating
ovens and stoves, and handling uncooked food. If children are assisting in the preparation of any
recipe, they should always be supervised by an adult.

Many of the designations used by manufacturers and sellers to distinguish their product are
claimed as trademarks. Where those designations appear in this book and F+W Media was aware of
a trademark claim, the designations have been printed with initial capital letters.

Cover image © 123rf.com/Maryana Teslenko.
Interior illustrations by Barry Littman.

This book is available at quantity discounts for bulk purchases.
For information, please call 1-800-289-0963.

Contents

Part II Growing Green Smoothie Vegetables and Herbs | 149

Part III Green Smoothies from the Garden | 203

Introduction
Tracy Russell

Why drink green smoothies? If you're like most people, you're probably concerned with your health. After every holiday season of indulging on waist-expanding goodies, you're ready to re-up your gym membership, knock off snacking between meals, and make a change in your diet.

All of those things are important to a healthy lifestyle, and drinking a green smoothie every day can have a huge impact on your life and your health. If you're consistent in this habit, you can lose anywhere from twenty to one hundred-plus pounds. You'll pleasantly surprise your doctor; she may even take you off blood pressure and cholesterol medications. In fact, some who choose to follow the green smoothie lifestyle are now running marathons because the smoothies have given them more energy and a zest for life than any diet program ever provided.

Countless scientific studies have shown a link between increased fruit and vegetable consumption and a lower risk of illness. Many fruits and vegetables have been studied for their protective effects against major diseases including cancer, cardiovascular disease, stroke, macular degeneration, Parkinson's, Alzheimer's, and many more ailments that plague us.

Green smoothies provide a delicious and fun way of ensuring that we all consume at least five or more servings of fruits and vegetables each and every day. Even if you hate the taste of spinach or kale, a green smoothie contains just enough sweet fruit to mask the flavor. Yes, it can actually be fun—and delicious—to drink kale! And no more chewing monotonous salads every day!

Green smoothies can revolutionize your health. But it is also important to use only the freshest, highest-quality fruits, berries, vegetables, and leafy greens. So much of the produce in grocery stores has been treated with pesticides and fungicides. You don't know exactly how the produce was handled, and increasingly frequent recalls on items like tomatoes, spinach, and leaf lettuce is worrisome.

So why not do away with those concerns by growing your own smoothie ingredients?

- There's the freshness. Once a fruit or vegetable has been picked, it starts to lose its vitamins and phytonutrients. Produce in the grocery store simply isn't at its peak of freshness (and nutrition), since it may have been harvested a week ago, or often longer.

- You can ensure that the lettuce, spinach, or cucumbers are truly organic and that they haven't been treated with any chemicals during growth or after harvest. And you won't have any question at all about the freshness and nutritional integrity of the food you feed yourself and your family.

- And there's cost. Grocery store vegetables can be expensive; by growing your own, you'll help the family budget as well as getting produce that tastes better than anything you can buy in the supermarket.

The way to get the absolute maximum nutritional benefits of your green smoothies is to grow a "green smoothie garden." Not only will you be able to harvest ingredients that you use in your green smoothie that very same day, you will also have complete control over how your produce is grown.

Creating a Green Smoothie Garden not only provides the opportunity to nourish your family with the best produce you can get but also reconnects you to your food. Growing your own food is not only fun and enjoyable, it just may give you the edge you need to live a long, happy, and healthy life—thanks to your homegrown green smoothies!

For more information on green smoothies, visit my website, Incredible Smoothies (*www.incrediblesmoothies.com*).

Good gardening and happy smoothies!

Part I

From Garden to Smoothie

Chapter 1
Why Plant a Smoothie Garden?

Green smoothies are a delicious and healthy way to supplement our diets, giving us the benefits of fruits and vegetables in intensive doses. The amazing powers of healing and the countless benefits from consuming rich greens used in smoothies are astounding. Abundant vitamins, minerals, antioxidants, amino acids, omega-3s, healthy fats, phytochemicals, and proteins that can change the natural processes of your body for the better are unleashed in every green smoothie you consume!

Now not only can you find improved health through smoothies; as well, in this book we'll show you how to grow the veggies you use in them. When you sit down to a delicious smoothie, you'll have the satisfaction of knowing that much of its ingredients came from your soil and was produced by your own hands. Homegrown vegetables are more flavorful than store-bought varieties. They don't contain preservatives or unhealthy chemical fertilizers. When you sip a green smoothie made from your own vegetables, not only will you be promoting a strong, healthy body but you'll also be participating in the growing small-farming movement, which is ecologically and economically important to the future of this country.

You don't need a big plot of land to grow the veggies for healthy green smoothies. A vegetable garden can be as small or as large as you want or need; it can be in a few pots on your balcony, a large acreage in the country, or any size in between.

✳ *Smoothie Garden Solution*

Gardening is good for your health! You can burn 150–250 calories per hour just by getting out into your vegetable garden. Exercise also releases endorphins into the bloodstream. Endorphins make you feel happy and give you a more positive outlook overall.

Planting a vegetable garden can be very rewarding. It is miraculous how a tiny little seed can produce enough vegetables to create the amazing smoothies you love.

Before you start, though, it is important to consider that gardening does take time, money, and energy. Be realistic when you estimate how much time you have to devote to your garden. People will often start a huge garden in the spring, only to tire of it and let the weeds take over by summer. If you are a first-time gardener, start small. Increase the size of your site every year as you become more familiar with growing your own vegetables.

If you only have a few minutes a day to spend on your vegetable garden, perhaps you can start with a few pots. If you have a few hours a week, you could manage a small garden spot or perhaps a raised bed. If you want to grow enough food to feed your family all year round, you may need to set aside at least one day a week to tend to a much larger garden. No matter where you live, you can find a spot to grow some of your own vegetables.

What Do You Want to Grow?

When choosing a garden site, it is important to know what you would like to grow. Some vegetables need warmth and lots of sunlight to grow, while others do well in a shadier spot. Of course, you also need to have some idea of what kind of smoothies you like and what veggies they call for. Therefore, you may want to take a look through the recipes listed in Part III of this book, see which ones sound especially appetizing, and plan your garden around them. Remember, you can always expand or change out vegetables in future gardening plans.

It is important to plan as inclusively as possible. Get your family involved so they can be part of the decision-making process. That way, they will feel a sense of ownership, and just might be more willing to help plant and take care of the garden. After all, they'll be drinking those smoothies too!

✳ Smoothie Garden Solution

Children love to garden. For young children, choose quick-growing veggies like peas so they can watch them grow. Veggies that are fun to eat, like carrots, are also great. Let older children grow what they want in their own designated little garden. Teach them how to plant, weed, water, and take care of that area. You can also extend that to the kitchen, letting them assemble the garden veggies they want in their smoothies.

Some vegetables take a lot more of your time than others, so take that into account when you make your selections. Lettuce varieties are easy to grow and can be harvested from just a few plants several times. A twenty-foot row of asparagus will take some time to plant initially, but you'll be able to look forward to enjoying asparagus in the spring for years to come. Some root crops such as carrots, beets, or garlic need to be thinned as they grow. This can be time-consuming, especially if you have large rows of these vegetables. It is important to know how much time you want to put into gardening.

If space is a consideration, research plants that give bigger yields but don't take up a lot of space. Root crops and leafy greens will yield a lot for the space they use up. You can train tomatoes, cucumbers, and beans to grow vertically, giving you more of a harvest for the space used. Consider growing vegetables that have more than one edible part. For example, if you grow beets, you'll find smoothie recipes later in this book that use both the beet itself and the greens.

Here is a list of common smoothie vegetables and herbs you can easily grow:

- Basil
- Beets
- Broccoli
- Carrots
- Cauliflower
- Celery
- Cilantro
- Cucumbers

- Garlic
- Green Onions
- Kale
- Lettuce
- Mint
- Parsley
- Peas

- Pepper, Assorted Colors
- Radicchio
- Romaine
- Spinach
- Watercress
- Zucchini

Growing a vegetable garden will take effort and time, so it is important to grow what you or your family will eat. (Naturally, you can use the contents of your garden in things other than smoothies.) Do not be afraid to try something new. A vegetable fresh from the garden has much more flavor than most veggies bought at the local grocery store, so you could be surprised by what you or your family will eat! If you find you do not like something or have an overabundance of certain veggies, give some away to friends, neighbors, or your community food bank.

Chapter 2
Making the Best Use of Your Space

It's possible that at this point you're thinking, I'd love to grow my own vegetables for smoothies, but I don't have the space for a garden. Don't worry—I'm going to show you how to use small spaces to maximum benefit. Before we get into the details, though, we need to think about some basic issues for any garden: climate, light, and water. Understanding the source of these three things and how they affect your smoothie garden will make all the difference.

Consider Your Climate

The United States and Canada are divided into plant hardiness zones that range from 1—the coldest areas such as Alaska—up to 11—the warmest areas, such as southern California, southern Florida, and Hawaii. These zones are based on temperature variations and first and last frost dates, which give the gardener an idea of what plants will grow best in each zone.

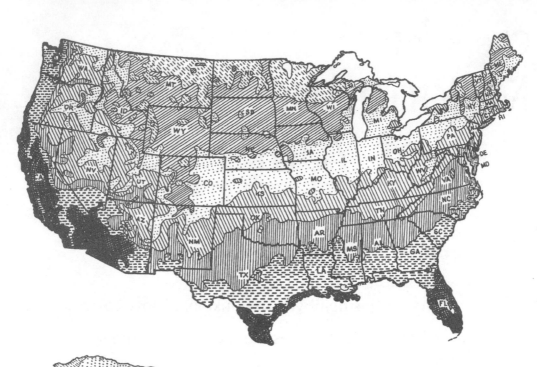

Range of average annual minimum temperatures for each zone

Zone 1	Below –50°F	
Zone 2	–50° to –40°	
Zone 3	–40° to –30°	
Zone 4	–30° to –20°	
Zone 5	–20° to –10°	
Zone 6	–10° to 0°	
Zone 7	0° to 10°	
Zone 8	10° to 20°	
Zone 9	20° to 30°	
Zone 10	30° to 40°	
Zone 11	Above 40°	

Planting zones in the United States

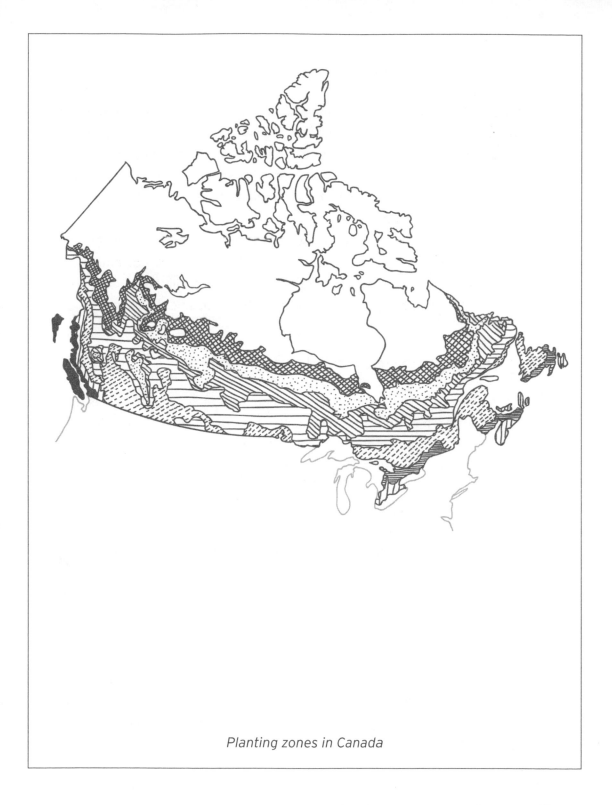

Planting zones in Canada

These zones can be important when choosing perennial plants, but most vegetable gardeners grow annuals within their area's growing seasons. Most areas in the United States and Canada also have four seasons—spring, summer, fall, and winter. The majority of gardeners grow vegetables in the spring and summer, although some gardeners in the southern United States can grow during the fall and winter months as well. Growing seasons can be extended by using greenhouses or other structures to give vegetable plants protection from inclement and unpredictable weather.

The length of your growing season will be pretty standard but can vary depending on the weather. You should also be aware of the average amount of rainfall in your area when choosing your site. The general climate of your area is important to consider, but each garden site will have specific issues.

The Importance of Sunlight

Sunlight plays a big part in growing a successful vegetable garden. This is the one area you have the least control over. When choosing your garden site, you will need to consider the amount of sunlight these areas get throughout the day. Most vegetables need an average of six hours of sunlight in order to grow. But don't fret if you only have a shadier spot. There are a few plants that will grow in a bit of shade, and perhaps you can grow other vegetables in containers that can be moved around to follow the sun's path.

The sun alters its path throughout the seasons, so take the time to track its progress. Jot down the time when sunlight hits your area throughout the different seasons and record how long it stays there. It may not matter if your smoothie garden site is deprived of sunlight in the winter because you won't be growing anything at that time, but if you get no sun during the spring and summer, you will need to choose another site.

You also want to consider how the trees in the area affect the amount of sun your site will receive. You may get full sun in the winter months when the leaves are off the trees, but the site becomes shadier as the leaves come out. The solution is to find a sunnier spot if you will be growing your veggies during the spring and summer.

The following vegetables do well with four to six hours of sunlight a day:

- Carrots
- Lettuce
- Kale
- Peas

Consider whether your vegetable plants will have any competition for the soil's nutrients. Perennial shrubs aren't usually a problem, and they can even benefit your garden by attracting beneficial insects to the vegetable patch. But beware of planting your garden near large trees, which will take nutrients from your vegetable plants.

✳ *Smoothie Garden Solution*

Choosing aged animal manures or compost or shredded leaves or seaweed does not really make a difference. What is most important is to add organic matter to your garden soil every year. Choose what is readily available and inexpensive so you can add large amounts to your beds.

Most gardeners do not have an ideal garden site; however, you can still grow a great vegetable garden with a little knowledge and a willingness to experiment with different vegetables. What books or seed catalogs say will or will not grow has been proven wrong in many garden sites.

The Water Source

The amount of rainfall your garden gets will vary from year to year, so a good water source near your garden site is essential. Most people will be less inclined to water if they have to carry it from a long distance away. Make sure your garden hose can easily reach across the full length of your garden site.

Most vegetable plants need one to two inches of water each week; some will need more if you live in an extremely hot climate. Containers and raised beds may also need more watering depending on the temperature in your area and how much rainfall you get. There are several different ways of watering your vegetable garden, including using sprinklers, a soaker hose, drip irrigation, and hand-watering.

Wooden raised beds

❊ *Smoothie Garden Solution*

Place small, empty tuna cans in four different areas of your vegetable garden. Turn on the overhead sprinkler and leave it on for one hour. Measure the amount of water in each can. This will give you an indication of how much water various spots in your garden receive from the sprinkler in an hour.

If you live in an area that gets a lot of rainfall, consider investing in a rain gauge. It will help you keep track of the amount of water your vegetable garden receives. If you get too little water, the vegetable plant roots won't be able to grow deep enough to reach the reserves of water and nutrients in the soil. Too much water will saturate the soil, reducing the amount of air space needed for the vegetable roots to grow strong, deep, and healthy. Either is harmful to your vegetable plants, and stressed plants will not produce as much.

Designing Your Site

Now that you know your climate zone and you've evaluated your sources of light and water, it is time to decide how you want to grow your vegetables. What space is available to you? Do you have a tiny balcony, porch, patio, or alleyway only big enough for a few pots? Or is the space a large patio that will enable you to have some larger planter boxes, perhaps to grow a dwarf fruit tree? Is the space fairly flat and rows will work best for you? Do you have poor soil and a raised bed would be the best option? These are all great ways to grow a fabulous vegetable garden. Consider the following design options to see what's best for you.

Container Gardening

If you live in the middle of a city and the only sunny area you have available is on a balcony, porch, or in some other small space, growing in containers is the perfect option to make a lovely vegetable garden. Containers come in various sizes and can sit or hang in your space. Some vegetables grow better in containers than others, so to get the best results possible, you want to be informed when choosing your vegetable plants.

In some urban homes or offices all the access you may have to the outdoors is a concrete patio. These are often areas that get a lot of sun. Sometimes these spots are a little too hot, but they might offer ideal conditions for growing your food using containers. Patios are usually big enough to accommodate larger planters, enabling you to easily grow larger vegetables and even some fruit trees and berry bushes.

Row Method

Row gardening is best used if you have a flat area. Even though row gardening is usually used on larger plots, this method of growing can be easily utilized in small spaces, such as in a flat sunny front or backyard. When planning a row garden, it is important to make sure you allow space for pathways between and at the end of each row to accommodate a place for you to walk and use any larger tools, like a rototiller or wheelbarrow. Walking on the soil where you will be planting your veggies can compact it and harm the soil structure. When designing this style of garden, make designated pathways.

Rows can be as long or as wide as you want or need them to be. Often the width is dependent on the type of equipment you will be using to till the beds. If you are going to be using a rototiller, measure the width of the tines. This will give you an idea of how wide you want your bed to be. When choosing the width of your garden bed, consider how long your reach is; if you are weeding on one side, can you easily reach across the bed without straining your back?

Growing in Raised Beds

Raised beds are structures that have four sides and hold soil. They are a great option for a small space, for areas with poor soil, for a hillside garden, or if you want structures in your garden. If you want to grow in a moist area that has poor drainage, the raised bed will allow for better drainage. If you have a sloped or terraced garden site, raised beds will help define these areas and make it easier to grow plants in the more difficult-to-reach areas. If the garden is replacing your front lawn and you want it to look attractive to your neighbors, using raised beds is a great way to add structure, definition, and tidiness to your vegetable garden. Raised beds are often used in community gardens, as they can be easily designated to individual growers.

Another great reason for using raised beds is that the bed can be made to any height. If you have physical disabilities, have limited mobility, or cannot bend easily, the raised bed can work very well for you. Make sure it is built to the height that works best for you. If it is a low bed, adding a ledge on the top will allow you to sit while gardening. And the ledge is great for older gardeners or those that cannot easily get down on hands and knees to plant or weed.

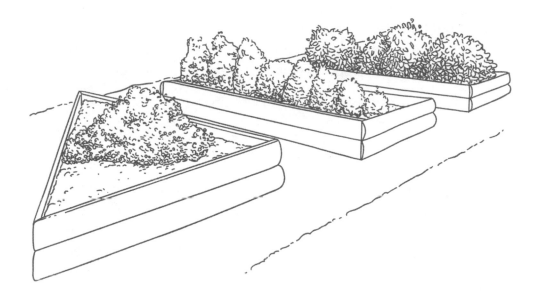

Raised beds can be made in any shape

✳ Smoothie Garden Solution

Save water by growing vegetables rather than having a green lawn. According to Environment Canada, a single lawn sprinkler spraying nineteen liters per minute uses more water in just one hour than a combination of ten toilet flushes, two five-minute showers, two dishwasher loads, and a full load of laundry.

If you choose to remove the sod from your front or backyard, start with one small area or build a raised bed to put over the sod. Removing sod can be time-consuming and hard work—and remember that you're inevitably removing some valuable soil when you remove the sod. One option is to turn the sod over, leaving it to decompose over several weeks. Another option is to use mulch to prevent the grass from getting sunlight, so it will die back naturally. This option will take longer to make a bed, but it's easier on the back!

Turn Your Lawn into a Smoothie Vegetable Garden

1. Cover the area you want to make into a vegetable garden with cardboard, overlapping the cardboard to make sure no area is left uncovered.

2. Moisten the cardboard by spraying it with water.

3. If you have any shredded leaves or grass clippings, put a one- to three-inch layer over the cardboard.

4. Place three to twelve inches of compost or garden soil on top of the whole area. If you can only put on a couple of inches, leave the site for a few weeks so the cardboard can decompose a bit. If you can add twelve inches of soil, you can start planting your seeds and transplants immediately.

You now have a garden site instead of a lawn. You can spruce up the area by adding trellises or other garden structures. If you are the first one in your neighborhood to turn your lawn into a vegetable garden, take the time to make it look great and share your harvest. Your neighbors may feel inspired to follow in your footsteps.

From Lawn to Garden

More and more people are replacing all or part of their lawns with vegetables and flowers. In a lot of areas, water restrictions mean you might have a brown lawn during the summer months. It's not very attractive, so why not put in a smoothie veggie garden instead?

If you are concerned about what your neighbors or community will say, take the time to tell them what you are planning to do. Make sure there are no restrictions; if there are, go to the town or neighborhood committee for permission. Growing your own food is important for all of us, and it has become fashionable as well.

City Gardening

Living in a rural or suburban setting where land is more readily available to grow your own vegetables gives you an advantage when starting a garden. What do you do if you live in an apartment building or condominium?

Balcony or Porch Gardening

Balcony or porch gardening is becoming increasingly common as more people want to grow some of their own vegetables. If you have a sunny spot to put a few containers, you have a garden site. Even if the area does not get full sun all day, many varieties of vegetables grow well in containers. The balcony is a great place to grow your smoothie vegetables vertically (which takes up less space), so consider growing plants that do well trellised. Try cucumbers and peas.

Condominium Gardening

Many condominiums have common spaces or even rooftops that would be perfect for growing vegetables. Talk with your condo board and suggest starting a vegetable garden in these common areas. A garden makes a wonderful space for people to relax and get together, and fresh food is a great bonus for everyone in the complex.

Community Gardens

A community garden is a shared space where a group of people or residents of a certain area grow their vegetables. More and more city neighborhoods are starting community gardens on empty lots in the center of a city, in local parks, and on private properties that are donated for this purpose. These gardens can be funded through local governments, community services, or specific groups. The main purpose is to make space available for growing food for everyone who wants to take part. If you are looking for a spot to grow on, check out your local area for an existing community garden or look into starting one in your neighborhood.

Community Supported Agriculture Garden (CSA)

A Community Supported Agriculture garden (CSA) is usually started by a farmer who decides to grow vegetables for a group of people who sign up to receive a certain amount of food each week during the growing season. Being a member of the CSA often means volunteering at the farm to help out with planting, weeding, and harvesting the vegetables. This is a great way for you and your family to spend a few days a month helping to grow the food you receive from the CSA every week. The website *www.localharvest.org/csa* allows you to find participating farms in your area. Of course, in a CSA many of the veggies you grow aren't ones you'll use in your smoothies. But they'll be delicious and healthy in many other recipes for your family table.

✳ *Smoothie Garden Solutions*

Even in the smallest garden, make room for a place for at least one person to sit. This adds purpose to the space and will be a lovely place to enjoy your garden. You can place your seating in a shady spot so you can relax after a hot day of working.

Your Soil

Now that you know where you're going to put your smoothie garden, you're ready to roll up your sleeves and get down and dirty. Specifically, you're ready to analyze your soil and do any prep necessary for it.

Fertile soil is a necessary element to a successful garden in the ground or in containers. Soil supports the vegetable plants by providing them with nutrients, warmth, air circulation, and the moisture they need to grow to maturity. Most gardens do not have ideal soil; however, with a little work and attention, you can develop healthy, fertile soil that your plants will love.

✳ Smoothie Garden Solution

When planting containers it is important to use a light soil mix or good compost. If you use soil from your garden, it is often too heavy and will not allow air to circulate in the container. Garden soil will impede the growth of your plants rather than support it.

Proper moisture is another very important ingredient needed in soil to support healthy plants. The water in the soil encases the soil particles and dissolves them; this enables the vegetable plant to absorb the nutrients through the water. If the soil gets too wet, it becomes saturated and does not leave any room for the oxygen and carbon dioxide to reach the plant roots or for the water to dissolve the soil particles. The plants are left nutrient-deficient. Your soil needs a healthy balance of soil particles, organic material, water, and air circulation so plants can get the oxygen, moisture, and nutrients needed to grow to maturity.

When used in containers, the soil has more restrictions. So a lightweight soil mix is important to allow proper movement of the water and air. This will ensure the plants get what they need.

Soil is made up of soil particles, organic matter, humus, water, and air. Soil particles are mineral materials that have been broken down into pieces smaller than pebbles. The organic matter and humus are made from decaying organisms, mainly plants that are at various stages of decomposition. About half of soil is actually solid; the rest is filled with air and water.

Air space is needed so that oxygen and carbon dioxide can move freely in and out of the soil; both are needed for vegetable plant roots to grow. Clay soil can impede airflow, as it is heavy and soil can get compacted by machinery or by being walked on. Either practice can inhibit good air circulation in the soil—another reason to have designated pathways to prevent your garden beds from becoming compacted.

The Four Basic Types of Soil

Now that you know more about what soil is and what your plants need to grow well, it is time to take a look at your own garden soil. Does it look healthy? Is it dark in color, rich-smelling, and crumbly, or is it hard, grayish in color, and dry? Are there earthworms when you dig around in it, or is it rocky with some straggly weeds? No matter what you are starting with there are always ways to improve it; soil is a living thing and will need amending and fertilizing along the way.

So what kind of soil do you have? There are four basic types: sand, silt, clay, and loam (sometimes called humus).

Sandy Soil

Sandy soil is mostly made up of sand and is the opposite of clay soil. Sandy soil is made up of large particles that do not hold together well. As a positive, sandy soil is often the warmest soil, which can benefit heat-loving vegetables. The main drawback to this type of soil is that it does not hold the water that is needed to move the nutrients from the soil to your plants. To tell if you have sandy soil or not, pick up a small handful and rub your fingers through it; if it falls apart and feels gritty, your soil is made mostly of sand.

To improve sandy soil you will need to add organic matter such as compost, rotted manures, and shredded leaves. Doing this every year, or even twice a year if you have enough material, is ideal. Organic matter adds nutrients to the soil and helps it to retain moisture. Both nutrients and moisture, which may be lacking in a sandy soil, are needed to grow healthy vegetable plants.

Clay Soil

In clay soil the particles are very tiny and bind together to make the soil heavy and difficult to work with. Another disadvantage is clay soil stays colder than other soils, so plants often have a tendency to grow slower. It also can get waterlogged and prevent oxygen from reaching the roots of your vegetable plants. On the positive side, clay soil is richer in nutrients and retains more moisture than sandy soil, which means it needs less water in the hot summer months. To check if you have clay soil, take a small handful of soil, add a little water, and roll it between your hands. If it forms an elongated shape and does not easily fall apart, you have mostly clay in your soil.

✳ *Smoothie Garden Solution*

Raised beds or containers are always great options if you have poor soil or live in an urban area where there is no open ground available. There are good packaged soil mixtures sold at garden nurseries. Be sure to consider the initial cost; however, raised beds or containers are great ways to grow some of your own veggies.

To improve clay soil, you want to add as much organic matter as you can. By adding in compost, shredded leaves, and rotted manures (such as horse, cow, or chicken manure), you will help to enlarge the amount of space between the soil particles and make the soil lighter. This will increase air circulation, allowing the oxygen and nutrients to be absorbed by the plants.

Silt Soil

Silt soil has medium-sized particles, larger than clay and smaller than sandy soils. Silt drains better than clay soil and holds nutrients better than sandy soils. This type of soil is very rare and is really only found near rivers or in areas that were once under water. The main disadvantage to silt soil is that it lacks organic matter, but that can be easily remedied by adding it in. To test if you have silty soil, put a small amount of soil in your palm, add a bit of water, and rub it between your fingers. Silty soil will have a soapy feel to it.

Loamy Soil

Loamy soil has the ideal soil structure, which is a mixture of sand, clay, and silt. It holds nutrients, retains moisture but does not get soggy, and it is easy to work with. Gardeners who have been gardening for years usually have made what soil they started with into a rich, loamy soil. A rich, loamy soil is slightly moist and crumbles easily by just poking your fingers into it. It is very similar to rich, well-rotted compost.

Most soils are a combination, just with a bit more sand or clay in them. But no matter what your soil type, it will need to be replenished with healthy amendments (organic materials) and organic fertilizers on a regular basis. Your vegetable plants are drawing nutrients continuously while they are growing. Rain and wind can wash or blow away nutrients as well, so it is important to know your soil and to take care of it in order to have healthy vegetable plants.

Drainage Concerns

The amount of moisture present in the soil plays a huge part in allowing nutrients to be used by the plants. Too much or too little water is a concern when trying to grow healthy veggie, fruit, and herb plants. If you have water sitting in your garden after a rain or if your water seems to drain away too quickly, you probably have a drainage problem. In containers, if the plants become waterlogged or dry out, their growth can be affected, so drainage holes in containers are extremely important for keeping your plants healthy.

✳ *Smoothie Garden Solution*

Nature's plants rely on fallen limbs, leaves, seeds, and eventually huge trees that decompose over time, making a forest a blanket of rich humus. High-fiber, woody materials are exactly what some soils need. Sawdust and wood chip mulch will conserve water, control weeds, and build long-term soil fertility.

Organic matter in soil helps to lighten it, offering better drainage and the ability to hold the correct amount of water for your plants. Add in as much organic materials as possible, such as compost or aged animal manure (several inches if you have that much), and till or dig it under. Mulching with straw or leaves can protect the soil from erosion and leaching of nutrients; the mulch will decompose over time, adding organic matter to the soil. With container gardens, it is important to renew your soil every year before planting a new crop, as well as regularly fertilizing every few weeks.

If your garden area has a drainage problem and you are not sure how to go about fixing it, call a landscaper to assess the situation for you. Drainage pipes, which can help remove any excess water you may have in your garden site, can be placed underground. Well-drained soil helps to keep plant roots from becoming waterlogged, allowing the plants to absorb the nutrients and oxygen needed to grow and mature. Poorly drained soil leaves your vegetable plants more susceptible to root rot and disease.

Backyard Composting

Welcome to the wonderful world of compost! For your smoothie vegetables to taste their best and grow in the healthiest way possible, you need to make compost for your plants. Making compost can be a huge benefit for your vegetable garden. It does take some work, but for a little time and effort, the rewards are great! A compost pile makes use of your kitchen waste that otherwise would go into the garbage, and is an excellent spot to recycle your weeds (just make sure they have not gone to seed). You can allow other garden debris to decompose in the pile rather than having it go to the landfill. Having a compost pile is also a great way to keep your garden clean. The resulting compost is perfect for using in your garden beds or containers.

✳ *Smoothie Garden Solution*

Shredded leaves will decompose much faster than whole ones (any tree leaves will work for mulch). Rake fallen leaves into a pile and then run your lawn mower over them. If you have a bag on your mower, that's even better because you can then just empty it into your compost pile or place the shredded leaves directly onto your garden bed as mulch.

Making a Compost Pile

The best times to make a new compost pile is in the spring or in the fall, as the heat of the summer or the cold in winter will not slow down the decomposition process. A good-size pile will most likely take from three to six months to decompose into good compost. The final result should be a rich, dark-colored material that smells earthy and easily crumbles in your hands.

To make your compost pile:

1. Lay down four to six inches of carbon material—for example, straw, shredded or dried leaves, small sticks, and corn or broccoli stalks (chopped into smaller pieces or put through a chipping machine, if possible).

2. Cover that with four to six inches of green material—for example, leaves, grass, and kitchen waste.

3. Add in a handful of organic fertilizer lime if you want.

4. Then cover with a thin layer of soil or animal manure to keep the flies and odor down.

5. Repeat these steps.

For best results, make the pile at least three feet high by three feet wide before leaving it to sit. Temperature is an important factor in making compost; the larger the pile, the easier it is for the material in it to get to the high temperatures needed to kill any weed seeds or diseased plant material. A temperature that is either too low or too high can slow down the decomposition process, while warm weather has a tendency to speed it up a bit. The pile usually starts out cool, and then as the materials start to decompose, the temperature inside the pile increases. Once your compost pile has reached approximately three feet by three feet, let that one sit and start a new pile. Most plastic compost bins will be approximately this size when they are full so you can move the bin, leaving the pile to work, or use two bins if you have a large amount of debris.

Choosing a Compost Bin

Constructing your own bin rather than purchasing one can save you money, as you can use recycled materials. Another benefit is that you can make it any size to fit your needs. A simple compost structure is a three-sided bin made by stacking concrete blocks, railroad ties, wooden boards, bales of straw, or pallets. Wire fencing or wire mesh can also be used to make a less solid bin so long as the holes are small enough to hold the materials you have. Bending the wire into a circular shape is often the easiest and the sturdiest shape to set up. Often, you can get these materials for free; they are also fairly inexpensive to purchase. Make sure the walls are about four feet high and the area inside is a minimum of three feet by three feet.

✳ *Smoothie Garden Solution*

When making compost, you want to have a balance of green and brown material. Too much green material will attract flies and give your compost a strong odor; too much brown material will slow down the decomposition of the pile.

Moisture is another important aspect to consider when making compost. The amount of moisture needs to be high, so make sure you add water to your compost regularly. Never let your compost pile dry out, especially in the summer months. Keeping the pile covered will keep the sun from drying it out as well as preventing the rain from making it too wet. Here's a way to check to see if your pile has the proper amount of moisture. Take a handful of compost from the middle of the pile, and if it is crumbling and slightly moist to the touch, there is enough moisture. If it forms a hard ball, the pile is too wet.

The moisture in the pile will allow air, which is also needed in the decomposing process, to filter in. Turning your pile will also allow more air circulation, and is especially important if your pile is too wet. A lot of gardeners never turn their compost and that method does work; however, taking the time to turn your pile over regularly will hasten the decomposition process.

Chapter 3
Vegetable Seeds for Your Smoothie Garden

A vegetable is a plant that is eaten whole or in part; often, the seed is eaten. The seed is also the part of the plant that produces a whole new vegetable plant. This chapter will provide you with great advice on how to choose your seeds for your smoothie veggies, the best ways to start them indoors or outdoors, and how to care for the seedlings as they grow. You will also learn how to save money by saving your own seeds for growing next season.

Choosing Seeds

Hybrids. Genetically modified seeds. Open pollination. Looking at all the choices in a seed catalog can be quite overwhelming. What do all those terms mean, and why are there ten different varieties of cucumbers?

First Things First

When purchasing seeds you will want to buy from a reputable seed company or exchange with friends. Look for local companies that grow trials of the vegetable seeds they sell. Your vegetables will be grown in a similar climate, which means you can be sure the seeds will do well in your garden.

Deciding on a Variety

Different vegetable varieties are created when plants naturally cross within a species or when researchers intentionally crossbreed. Some have shorter or longer maturity dates, some grow larger than others, and some do better in different temperatures. Seed catalogs will indicate some of the benefits of each variety. Take the time to read and choose the variety that will work best for your situation.

A hybrid variety is made when seeds from two parent plants are crossed for the purpose of improving the plant's productivity. Vegetable plants are often hybridized in order to create disease-resistant varieties and to increase vegetable size, color, and shape. Unfortunately, the seeds cannot be saved for future use. The seeds of a hybrid plant will not grow or will produce an inferior plant. If you are planning to save your own seeds, do not plant any hybrid varieties.

✳ *Smoothie Garden Solution*

Genetically modified seeds (GMO) are produced by manipulating genetic components from unrelated organisms with the idea of producing a better product. There are many concerns and very little testing for the health ramifications of GMO seeds. Organic gardeners recommend against purchasing or planting these seeds.

An open-pollinated seed is one where two parent plants from the same variety produce seeds, which in turn combine to produce a new plant just like the parent one. The male and female plants need to cross in order to create a new seed. Pollination is usually facilitated by insects, birds, or the wind, but it can be done by hand as well. If you choose open-pollinating varieties, you'll be limited to a single variety of those particular vegetables. Cross-pollination may occur if you plant multiple varieties, and the resulting plants may look and taste inferior to the parent vegetables.

Starting Seeds Outdoors

There are two ways to plant your smoothie vegetable seeds: directly outdoors into the soil or indoors in seed trays to be transplanted to the garden later. Different vegetable seeds have different requirements for germination and maturing; some need heat and some do better in cool weather. You must know the best way to start each of your vegetables. Most vegetable seeds will do well either way, but some vegetables, such as root crops, need to be seeded directly because they do not grow well if their roots are disturbed.

Starting seeds indoors will give them a head start. This is beneficial, especially if you live in a cold climate where you cannot get into your garden until the end of May.

Vegetables best started by seeding directly into the soil include:

- Beans
- Beets
- Carrots
- Garlic
- Peas
- Radicchio
- Romaine
- Spinach

✳ *Smoothie Garden Solution*

How deeply should the seeds be planted? Vegetable seed packets give you valuable information, such as how deep to plant each variety. However, if you don't have the seed packet handy, a good rule of thumb is to plant the seed twice the depth of the size of the seed.

When starting your seeds outdoors, make sure the conditions are right for your specific vegetable seed. If the soil is too wet and cold or too dry and hot, the seed may not germinate. Know what each variety of seed you are planting requires.

Here is a quick checklist for planting your seeds directly into your garden beds:

- ❑ Make sure the soil is moist.

- ❑ Mark the row using a stick, the edge of a hoe, or your finger. It should be the depth recommended for that particular seed.

- ❑ Sow the seed. If the seed is small, take a pinch of seed with your fingers and then gently spread the seed in the area you marked. Larger seeds can be dropped into the row. Place them an appropriate distance apart as you go.

- ❑ Cover the seed. You can gently cover the seed with soil by using your hand or the back side of a rake.

- ❑ Firm the soil down. This is done using your hand or the back of a hoe. This prevents the soil and seed from being blown away by wind or getting washed away when you water the bed.

- ❑ Water the bed. Seeds need to be moist to germinate, so gently spray the area you have just planted with water. Do not water too heavily or quickly or you may wash the seeds away. You will need to keep the area well moistened until you see the first green shoots coming through the soil, then water as needed. Do not let the bed dry out.

- ❑ Thin the plants. Once the first green shoots appear, some vegetable plants such as carrots, radishes, turnips, spinach, and salad greens need to be thinned. Thinning helps to make room for the vegetable plants to grow to maturity.

Some vegetables are difficult to start outdoors because the seed needs a very specific temperature to germinate. These are best started indoors so you have more control over their growing conditions. Some examples are tomatoes, peppers, and eggplants.

Transplants: Buy or Start Your Own?

Starting your own seedlings can be a very satisfying part of vegetable gardening. Its advantages are many. It can be more economical, especially if you have a large garden, and it gives you a head start with your growing season. You'll also know exactly how many plants you will have to transplant out, and you can prevent unwanted disease or pests from coming into your garden.

Buying Transplants

If you do not have the time or desire to start you own seedlings, check your local nursery or garden center for vegetable transplants. Make sure you purchase your seedlings from a reputable business and choose their healthiest seedlings. Unhealthy transplants can easily introduce insects and disease to your garden. A healthy transplant is bushy and compact, not spindly or leggy. The stems should be a healthy color and strong. Avoid plants whose roots are showing through the drain holes. These plants may be root bound, which may prevent them from growing to their full potential. Make sure you are ready to plant your transplants into the garden as soon as you bring them home.

Starting Your Own Seedlings

The process of starting your own seedlings can be intimidating, but it can be easily accomplished with a little know-how. Smoothie vegetables that do better started indoors and then transplanted to the garden include:

- Cauliflower
- Celery
- Lettuces
- Onions
- Peppers

Many nurseries or garden stores sell seed starter kits. They come with all the components needed to start your own transplants—a tray, cells, labels, and a clear plastic lid. The two most common sizes are sheets that have seventy-two cells and sheets with twenty-four cells. The larger the vegetable plants at maturity, the larger the flat you should use for growing the seedling. For example, lettuce is usually planted in the seventy-two-cell sheets and brassicas or tomatoes are started in the twenty-four-cell sheets. The tray, cells, and lid can be reused from year to year, but make sure they are clean. Use one part bleach to ten parts water to clean them at the beginning of the season.

Some kits come with a starter mix, but you may have to purchase this separately. Use sterile potting soil made specifically for starting seeds; it is lighter weight than your garden soil.

✳ *Smoothie Garden Solution*

Make sure the water you use on your young seedlings is at room temperature. Water straight from a tap or outdoor water barrel may be too cold for the transplants. If the roots get too chilled, they will not grow well.

To start your seeds indoors, fill the cells with the starter mix, making sure they are filled to the top, and gently firm each hole down with your fingers. Place the cell sheet into the tray, which is used to support the sheet and hold any water that may drain out of the bottom of the cells. Make small indentations in each cell using the tip of your finger or a pencil-size dowel, then place the seed inside it. Planting two seeds in each cell will give you a better chance of germination. If both germinate, cut the second seedling off with small scissors. Do not pull out the second seedling because this may damage the roots of the one you want to keep.

Once you have placed seeds in each cell, cover them with a light covering of the starter mix and gently firm the soil in each cell. Water gently and keep the soil moist until the seeds have pushed through the soil. Once they have sprouted, make sure your vegetable seedlings get full sunlight and the cells are watered regularly. Do not let the cells dry out; this is hard on the seedling and it will take a long time for the soil to absorb more water, which can stress the plant even more.

Some vegetables will need extra heat to germinate. You can purchase a heating pad from your local garden center or use a hotbed.

Caring for Your Seedlings

Now that you have your seeds planted in trays or directly in the ground, how do you care for them?

Common Quandaries

The seeds need to be kept moist for them to germinate, but the challenge of growing seeds outdoors is excessive rainfall. Too much moisture can saturate the soil, which can prevent the seeds from germinating or cause them to rot. If the temperature is too warm, the soil can become dry and hard, which prevents the sprouting seed from breaking through the soil. You will need to take extra care of your seeds and seedlings in the first few weeks after planting them; once they get established they will need less of your attention.

Growing indoors gives you more control over how much water the seeds get, but they need constant attention and often need to be watered at least twice a day if the weather is warm. If your seedlings are thin and breaking off at the base, this may be a sign of a soil-borne fungus called *dampening off*. If the seedlings are large enough to be transplanted, bury the stem as deep as possible. If the seedlings are still too young to go out into the garden, you will need to throw these in the garbage and start over again using clean cells.

Seeds do not need light to germinate, but once they have broken through the surface they need as much light as possible. Most seedlings need six hours of light to grow well. If you are starting them in late winter when the days are still short, grow lights may be necessary. Leggy and spindly looking seedlings may not be getting enough light. Another concern is extreme temperatures.

Young seedlings can burn and wilt very easily in the heat, and can die if they get too cold. Protecting them from extreme temperatures is necessary.

✳ Smoothie Garden Solution

What should you do if your seeds haven't sprouted? Don't panic. Some seeds, such as brassicas and lettuce, germinate quickly—sometimes in as few as four days. Others, such as onions, can take up to twenty-one days to germinate. Check to see how long the seed is supposed to take before you start worrying. If your seeds should have sprouted by now, seeds may be old and may not be viable anymore. Try planting again using fresher seeds.

Young seedlings are tender and tasty, making them more susceptible to some pests. One common concern for outdoor seedlings is slugs. If the leaves of your young lettuce or spinach plants are being eaten, you may have slugs. If the same thing is happening to your indoor seedlings, you may have a mouse problem. Part of caring for your seedlings is taking the time to observe them. If you find something wrong, investigate to find out what is happening to your plants.

Transplanting Your Indoor Seedlings

If you have decided to purchase your transplants, make sure you place them into the ground within a day or so of bringing them home from the nursery. If you started some of your own transplants, they will be ready to go into the garden after four to twelve weeks depending on the variety. The seedlings should have at least four true leaves before you set them out, and the outdoor soil temperature needs to be warm enough to support your vegetable plants.

It is important to transition some seedlings like tomatoes or peppers from being inside to being outside. They need to be set outside during the day and brought back in at night; gradually extend the time they are outside over several days. This is called *hardening off*.

Here is a checklist for setting out your transplants:

❑ Make sure the cells are moist before they are planted.

❑ Gently massage the seedling out of the cell, trying not to disturb the roots too much. Try not to tear the cell so you can reuse it next season.

- [ ] Make a hole the depth of the cell and place the transplant into it. Cover it with soil and firmly press the soil around the base of the plant.

- [ ] Water the transplant after planting. Remember the roots are tiny and close to the surface; water regularly so the soil does not dry out.

- [ ] Protect the plant from too much heat or cold so it can get a good start.

Choosing the right seed and making sure the seedling gets the best start will go a long way. A little care and attention in the beginning of a plant's life will give you a much healthier vegetable plant and a more abundant harvest.

Saving Seeds

When planning your garden layout, think about planting some vegetables for saving the seeds in the fall. This means you allow the plant to fully mature and then harvest the seed, saving it for planting next season. Some vegetable plants, such as peas and beans, produce pods with the seed inside. Others, such as tomatoes and cucumbers, produce fruit that contains the seeds. Still others, such as lettuce and onions, produce seed after they flower. And with vegetables such as potatoes and garlic, the root becomes the seed.

Beware of Hybrids

Seeds that will not cross-pollinate with each other are easy to save. However, if you have two different varieties of the same vegetable plant growing in the same area, you risk cross-pollination. A home gardener does not want to raise hybrid varieties for seed because hybrid seeds will not produce vegetables that are as good as their parents' seeds produced. These plants need to be isolated if you want to harvest the seeds. The degree of isolation depends on the plants. Some, such as peppers and eggplants, only need to be about fifty feet apart so they do not cross-pollinate. Others, such as corn, spinach, squash, and radishes, need total isolation. You should only plant one variety of these vegetables if you are planning on saving the seeds.

Commercial growers like to plant hybrid seeds because they are specifically created to produce similar-size crops that mature at the same time. This is great if you are selling your produce, but for a home gardener who only wants one plant to be ready at a time, choosing nonhybrid is a better option. You want to make sure you collect the seeds before they start dispersing naturally. You have to take the time to observe the plants to know when the seed is ripe enough for collecting, and you want to be sure you do it before they are blown away by the wind.

✳ *Smoothie Garden Solution*

Remember to label your seeds. Take the time to write down the vegetable type, variety, any special features, and the place and date you collected the seeds on the seed packet. The last thing you want to find is a whole box of unlabeled seeds.

Storing Your Seeds

The seeds must be thoroughly dry. Spread the seeds out on a plate or tray and place them in a warm location out of direct sunlight. Leave them for a couple of weeks to dry thoroughly. Before you put them into packets, make sure they are clean. Remove any chaff or dirt from the seed by placing the seeds into a kitchen sieve with holes tiny enough for just the chaff—not the seeds—to fall through. Try gently blowing on the seeds to remove any chaff.

Place your seeds in airtight containers. Plastic yogurt containers and paper envelopes work well. Keep them in a cool, dry spot such as a refrigerator or a cool, dry storage room. The main reason seeds do not last is because they become moldy or rot, both of which are caused by extreme changes in temperature or humidity.

Most seeds will last two to four years if saved and stored properly. If you are not sure whether your seeds are still good, it's easy enough to test their viability. Spread ten seeds on a damp paper towel. Place the towel and the seeds into a resealable plastic bag and seal it. Put the closed bag in an area out of direct sunlight—the top of your refrigerator is a good spot. Check back in four to ten days to see how many seeds sprouted. This will give you an indication of the percentage of seeds that will sprout if you plant them in your garden.

Whether or not you choose to save your own seeds, it is important to know how. There is more and more concern about how vegetable seeds are being grown and stored. If every home gardener chose to save only one variety of vegetable, it would make a difference. Start a seed bank in your community so you can support your fellow gardeners and the environment, and save yourself some money by sharing the seeds.

Chapter 4
The Care and Feeding of Your Smoothie Garden

There are many aspects to vegetable gardening. First you have to plan your garden, decide what you want to plant, and plant the seed. Then comes caring for the seed so it will germinate. And finally, you must keep your smoothie veggies happy all season long. In this chapter you will learn about a number of measures that can go a long way toward providing you with a successful smoothie vegetable harvest.

Crop Rotation

Crop rotation is a process that is used to ensure you do not plant the same vegetable or family of vegetables in the same spot in successive years. By moving your vegetables to a new spot each year, you will be able to keep the soil more fertile, reduce the amounts of pests and diseases in your garden, and ultimately have a healthier and more productive vegetable harvest. Crop or vegetable rotation may seem complicated when you first learn about it, but it can be easy.

Different vegetable plants use varying amounts of nutrients from the soil to grow well. You already know that you should add organic matter and fertilizer to your soil every year, but it is also important to move your plants around so you don't deplete the soil's nutrients. One year you may grow a vegetable that uses a lot of nitrogen, and the following year you may plant a crop that uses more phosphorus. Rotating the crops gives the soil time to rebuild the nitrogen in that area.

Crop rotation also helps you cut down on pests and diseases in your garden. A few of these little guys can wreak havoc on your vegetable patch, so it's in your best interest to keep them out. Certain vegetable plants will attract certain pests and diseases, which often live in the soil where the plant grows. By moving these vegetable plants to another area of the garden, you deprive the pests or diseases of their food. On the other hand, some plants repel certain pests and diseases, which will also help to keep them at bay.

❋ Smoothie Garden Solution

Flowers are a great way to add beauty to your vegetable garden and attract beneficial insects—and some flowers are even edible. Bee balm, pansies, nasturtiums, geraniums, tulips, violas, lavender, hollyhock, dianthus, daylilies, and roses are all edible and easy to grow. Harvest blooms just before using them.

To implement crop rotation in your garden, first divide your garden site into four fairly equal areas—five if you are planning to grow some perennial vegetables like asparagus or artichokes. You will plant a certain family of vegetables in each spot one year and move it clockwise to the next spot the following year. This will give you a four-year crop rotation. It is important to write down or draw a sketch of your garden so you have something to refer back to when planning for next season.

ROTATION CHART

	YEAR 1	YEAR 2	YEAR 3	YEAR 4
BED 1	Brassicas: broccoli, cauliflower, Brussels sprouts, kale	Heat-loving veggies: tomatoes, cucumbers, peppers, eggplants, basil	Root crops: carrots, potatoes, beets	Other crops: lettuce, peas, beans, chard, Oriental vegetables
BED 2	Heat-loving veggies: tomatoes, cucumbers, peppers, eggplants, basil	Root crops: carrots, potatoes, beets	Other crops: lettuce, peas, beans, chard, Oriental vegetables	Brassicas: broccoli, cauliflower, Brussels sprouts, kale
BED 3	Root crops: carrots, potatoes, beets	Other crops: lettuce, peas, beans, chard, Oriental vegetables	Brassicas: broccoli, cauliflower, Brussels sprouts, kale	Heat-loving veggies: tomatoes, cucumbers, peppers, eggplants, basil
BED 4	Other crops: lettuce, peas, beans, chard, Oriental vegetables	Brassicas: broccoli, cauliflower, Brussels sprouts, kale	Heat-loving veggies: tomatoes, cucumbers, peppers, eggplants, basil	Root crops: carrots, potatoes, beets

If you are growing your veggies in containers, either wash the container and change the soil each year or plant the veggie in a different pot each year. This will help to keep your container vegetables healthier.

Companion Planting

Certain vegetables have a positive effect on each other, and planting them close together can help you maximize the benefit. On the other hand, beware of plants that negatively affect each other; be sure to plant these in different parts of your garden.

Planting a certain group of vegetables with another can create a habitat for beneficial insects, which will help control the more harmful ones. Some vegetable scents will mask or hide a certain vegetable so pests will not be able to find it. Another plant may produce an odor that will repel certain pests or diseases. Certain plants are not affected by a certain pest or disease but will draw it away from a plant that is.

COMPANION PLANTING CHART			
	VEGETABLE	POSITIVE EFFECT	NEGATIVE EFFECT
ASPARAGUS	Parsley, tomatoes	Onions	
BEANS	Beets, borage, cabbage, carrots, cauliflower, corn, marigolds, squash, strawberries, tomatoes		Chives, fennel, garlic, leeks
BEETS	Cabbage, kohlrabi	Runner beans	
BROCCOLI	Beans, celery, dill, nasturtiums, onions, oregano, potatoes, rosemary, sage	Lettuce, strawberries, tomatoes	
BRUSSELS SPROUTS	Beans, celery, dill, nasturtiums, potatoes, rosemary, sage	Strawberries	
CABBAGE	Beans, beets, celery, dill, nasturtiums, onions, oregano, potatoes, rosemary, sage	Grapes, strawberries, tomatoes	

COMPANION PLANTING CHART			
	VEGETABLE	POSITIVE EFFECT	NEGATIVE EFFECT
CARROTS	Beans, leeks, onions, peas, radishes, rosemary, sage, tomatoes	Dill	
CAULIFLOWER	Beans, beets, celery, dill, nasturtiums, onions, oregano, potatoes, radishes, sage	Strawberries, tomatoes	
CELERY	Beans, cabbage, leeks, onions, tomatoes	Carrots, parsnips	
CORN	Beans, melon, peas, squash		
CUCUMBERS	Beans, broccoli, celery, Chinese cabbage, lettuce, peas, radishes, tomatoes	Sage, rue	
EGGPLANTS		Peas, tarragon, thyme	
KOHLRABI	Beets, onions	Beans, peppers, tomatoes	
LEEKS	Carrots, celery	Broad beans, broccoli	
LETTUCE	Beets, cabbage, clovers, peas, radishes, strawberries		
ONIONS	Beets, cabbage, carrots, lettuce, potatoes, strawberries, tomatoes	Beans, peas	
PEAS	Carrots, corn, cucumbers, eggplants, lettuce, radishes, spinach	Tomatoes, turnips, rutabagas	

COMPANION PLANTING CHART			
	VEGETABLE	POSITIVE EFFECT	NEGATIVE EFFECT
PEPPERS	Basil, carrots, lovage, marjoram, onions, oregano	Fennel, kohlrabi	
POTATOES	Beans, cabbage, corn, lettuce, onions, petunias, marigolds, radishes	Apples, pumpkins, tomatoes	
PUMPKINS	Beans, corn, nasturtiums, radishes	Potatoes	
RADISHES	Beans, cabbage, cauliflower, cucumbers, lettuce, peas, squash, tomatoes	Grapes, hyssop	
SPINACH	Cabbage, celery, eggplants, onions, peas, strawberries		
SUMMER SQUASH	Beans, corn, mint, nasturtiums, radishes	Potatoes	
TOMATOES	Asparagus, basil, cabbage, carrots, onions, parsley, peas, sage	Fennel, potatoes	
TURNIPS	Peas		
WINTER SQUASH	Beans, corn, mint, nasturtiums, radishes		
ZUCCHINI	Beans, corn, mint, nasturtiums, radishes	Potatoes	

Protecting Your Plants

Some vegetable plants need more care than others. Young seedlings or transplants are often the most vulnerable to weather extremes and pests. Different plants at various stages of their growth may need protection from the cold, frost, heat, excessive rain, or pests. A change in temperature—even if it's only a drop of a few degrees—can be harmful to your veggie plants. Cold weather, pests, or disease can kill a whole row of veggies in one night, so protecting them is important.

To have a successful garden, you need to take time to observe your veggie plants and be aware of the weather, especially in the spring when the temperature can vary widely from day to night. Most vegetable plants do not like the cold weather, and young plants can be quite fragile. To complicate matters, cold soil is more susceptible to fungi and disease, so it is important to protect the soil and plants if you live in a cold climate. Excessive heat can also kill your vegetable plants. The heat or dryness can make them wilt, which can cause them to become stunted or die if they are not attended to fairly quickly. Too much water can actually prevent your vegetable plants from getting the nutrients they need to grow well. For all of these reasons, you should always have materials near your garden so you can quickly cover or shield your plants.

✳ *Smoothie Garden Solution*

When "chewing pests" like slugs have assaulted your vegetable plants, the plants can generally handle up to 20 percent damage without a huge loss of yield or a negative impact on the quality of the harvest. The only exceptions are plants that are grown for their leaves, such as spinach or cabbage.

You probably already have all the materials you need to protect your vegetable plants from cold, heat, wind, bugs, birds, and other pests. The following list includes common items and how you can use them:

- **Cardboard box.** Place the box over a plant to keep it from getting too cold at night.

- **Metal cans.** Large tomato cans or coffee cans are ideal to protect a plant from the cold or pests. Remove both ends of the can and place it gently over the plant. You can leave the can on during the day; the sun will still be able to reach the plant.

- **Wooden boards.** Pieces of wood can be used to block excessive wind or sun.

- **Paper bags.** Place a paper bag over a young seedling to protect it from the cold. Wind can blow a bag away and rain can cause it to disintegrate, so only use this method on cold, clear nights.

- **Plastic containers.** Yogurt containers, milk jugs, and large water bottles can protect young seedlings from the cold or even from slugs. Remove both ends of the container and firmly place it into the soil around the young plant to prevent slugs from reaching the plant. A clear plastic container can be used as a mini greenhouse for plants that like a little extra warmth; just be careful not to let the plants get too hot.

- **Sheets.** Throw your old bed sheets over your vegetable patch on a cold spring night. They are light enough that they won't damage the plant, yet they will still provide adequate protection.

- **Plastic sheeting.** Plastic sheeting is best used over a structure of either wood or plastic hoops to protect your plants. Create a greenhouse or cold frame to protect your plants.

- **Floating row covers.** This material can be easily purchased at any garden center or from most seed catalogs. It is lightweight and will let in some light and water while it protects your plants from the heat, cold, and pests. It is light enough to be laid directly over your plants or it can be attached to plastic or wooden poles to make a shelter.

- **Fencing.** A fence is one way of protecting your whole garden from animals such as cats, dogs, deer, raccoons, and bears. If you live in an area where these animals are common, investing in a good fence will save you a lot of heartache. Different types of fencing are used for different types of animals.

Trellis and Staking

Some vegetable plants need support to grow and produce healthy fruits or pods. Tomatoes and cucumbers do best if they can grow upright so that the fruit is not lying on the ground and the plant can receive both light and air circulation. Some varieties of peas and beans can grow up to six feet high or more and need support. These climbing vegetables have vines that need to be able to attach to a structure of some sort in order to continue to grow taller.

It is important to know which plants will need staking or a trellis so that you can put these up just before you plant the seed or set out your transplants. If you wait, you can disturb the roots, which can cause stress, and the vines of different plants can grow into each other, making it difficult to place a stake or trellis without damaging the plant.

✳ *Smoothie Garden Solution*

If you have a small garden site, save space by growing a climbing vegetable next to a plant that has a sturdier stalk. Cornstalks make a great support for pole beans. You save space by growing them together and you save money by not having to make a support structure.

Growing vertically can save a lot of space, especially if you have a tiny garden site or grow in containers on your balcony. The plants are often healthier because they don't touch the wet or cold ground, and therefore attract fewer pests and diseases. Mildew and rot are common problems for many fruiting vegetables, so it's to your advantage to keep the fruit off the ground. When your plants grow upright, you can easily see the fruit to harvest. Gardening can be backbreaking work, but harvesting off an upright structure is easier on your body!

Trellis and staking material can be purchased at most garden centers or from seed catalogs. You can also make structures of your own out of materials you have on hand. The following is a list of some common types of trellises and stakes:

- **Plastic or nylon netting.** The plant's tendrils wind around the netting and move upward as they grow taller. The netting material is soft and easy to work with and will not decay. It can be cut to any size and is easily washed and stored. White nylon netting has large six-inch openings and is used mainly for larger plants like cucumbers and zucchini. Green plastic mesh netting has smaller openings, making it a better option for peas or beans. These trellis materials need to be supported by some kind of frame.

- **Wooden frame.** You can use scrap pieces of wood, bamboo, small tree branches, or even an old window frame to build a support for your netting. Make sure the frame is secure in the ground and attach the netting to the top and bottom of the frame with string, nails, or staples. Make sure the netting is fairly tight so it will support the weight of your plant when it starts to fruit.

- **Wooden stakes.** Wood, bamboo, or even small cut trees will all work well as sturdy stakes. The stakes must be secured far enough into the ground to give enough support. One foot in the ground for every three feet above ground is a good rule of thumb. Tie tomato plants to the stakes with string, pieces of cloth, or even old pantyhose.

- **Teepee structure.** You can use pieces of wood, bamboo, or sturdy tree branches to make your teepee. Take six stakes of equal length. Push each stake securely into the ground in a small circle, angling them all inward toward each other. The top of each stake should touch the others. Tie them together with a piece of string or twine. This is a great way to grow climbing beans and peas; just plant four to six seeds around the base of each pole and watch them grow.

Compost and Manure Teas

Organic fertilizer teas are a great way to replace nutrients in the soil so your smoothie vegetable plant roots can absorb and use them. These teas can also deter some pests if the plant's leaves are sprayed with a diluted mixture; just remember to wash the plant thoroughly before you eat it.

Most plants do better with an extra boost of nutrients at some point in their growth. Giving your young transplants some fertilizer tea when they are first set out in the garden will help reduce the shock of any root disturbance. Other vegetable plants need an extra boost of nutrients when they start to flower to encourage them to produce lots of fruits or pods.

Compost, animal manure, and comfrey are all great organic materials for making your fertilizer tea. Gardeners often have limited amounts of compost and animal manure, so they really do not have enough to put on all their garden beds.

✳ *Smoothie Garden Solution*

Write it down! When it comes to fertilizing your veggies, make sure you keep records. Keep a journal or notebook and jot down when you gave your plant fertilizer and how much was given. If you do not write it down, you may forget some plants and fertilize others too often.

Regularly fertilizing your plants and replenishing nutrients in your soil help keep them healthier. This reduces the risk that your plants will succumb to pests and diseases.

Make Your Own Compost or Manure Tea

You'll need a bucket or garbage can with a lid, hot animal manure or compost, and water. Follow these steps to make your tea:

1. Fill your bucket or garbage can one-third full with compost or manure and then fill it the rest of the way with water.

2. Mix well, cover, and let it sit at least overnight; letting it sit for a few days can make it stronger.

3. Put the tea directly around your plants or fill your watering can with half tea and half water to dilute it. If you dilute your tea, strain the tea with a piece of cheesecloth so you won't plug the nozzle on your watering can. This mixture can also be used to spray your plant leaves to deter pests.

4. Keep refilling your bucket or garbage can with more water until the water no longer turns dark brown. Once this happens, put the sludge into your compost and make a new batch of tea with fresh manure or compost.

Green Manures and Cover Crops

You can grow certain green plants, usually in the fall, and then cut and till them into the soil the following spring. This kind of plant is usually called a cover crop. Green manure is an easy and economical way of adding organic matter to the soil. As the green matter decomposes, it adds texture and nutrients back into your soil. A cover crop will:

• Enhance the soil structure and drainage

• Protect bare soil from being blown away by the wind

• Keep important nutrients from being leached away by rain

• Loosen the soil

• Help control weeds

• Help break pest cycles

• Provide you with your own mulch and compost material

Vetch, fava beans, winter field peas, clover, and fall rye can be grown to increase the nitrogen content in your soil. They are called *nitrogen fixers*, which means their roots will hold nitrogen and then release it into the soil once the plant is tilled under. Buckwheat and phacelias are often used to suppress weeds and are great to plant if you are just starting a new garden site or your old site has gotten overgrown with weeds.

You can plant a cover crop at any time, but most gardeners plant theirs after they have harvested their main crop. Before planting, make sure the bed is clean. Roughly rake over the area in order to break up the first few inches of soil. Then broadcast the seed and keep it well watered if the weather is warm and dry.

It is easiest to turn over a cover crop if the plants are not too high, so dig them in once they reach six to eight inches high. If they grow taller, cut the plant a few inches from the soil and use the material as mulch or put it into your compost. Till the crop under and leave it to decompose for a few weeks before you begin to plant any vegetables.

Easy Ways to Water

Your smoothie veggies need water to grow, mature, and produce fruits, pods, or seeds for you to enjoy. The amount of water each plant requires depends hugely on your climate, your soil, and the type of vegetable. All of these variables make watering a complex subject. Below you will learn about the benefits and disadvantages of the various ways you can water your garden. We will discuss hand-watering, overhead watering, and drip irrigation, and explain how to watch for signs that your plants may be in trouble.

Hand-Watering

Hand-watering is done by using a container such as a watering can or a hose connected to a water source to water individual vegetable plants. When choosing to hand-water, it is important that your water source is nearby. The main benefits of hand-watering include your ability to direct where the flow of water goes and to control when and how much water you give the plants. It also gives you the valuable opportunity to observe your plants. And the equipment you need is inexpensive to purchase.

Any kind of container that will hold water can be used to water your plants, but watering cans are probably the most common and are all fairly inexpensive. There are several different kinds of watering cans you can choose from, but the nozzle is the most important component. Each nozzle has a different number and size of holes, which can affect how much and how quickly the water comes out. If you are watering tiny seedlings, you want a nozzle that will give a light spray of water—a Haws watering can is great for this. If you are watering larger plants, the holes can be bigger to give a heavier spray of water.

If you choose to water with a hose, you must again consider the nozzle. Choosing one that has a variety of spray options is best. That allows you to give a lighter or heavier spray depending on what kind of plant you are watering. Making sure your hose easily reaches all areas of your garden site will make it easier for you to water regularly.

✳ Smoothie Garden Solution

Water is crucial for seed germination and seed growth, so it is important to keep your seedbed moist until the seeds have germinated. When setting out your transplants, make sure the seedlings are moist when planted and water again after planting. Young seedlings have very shallow roots, so you do not want the soil to dry out.

Some plants do better if you hand-water them. For example, containers are best hand-watered and there is less waste than using a sprinkler. Larger vegetable plants such as broccoli, cabbages, and cauliflower do better with hand-watering; if you use an overhead sprinkler to water them, the leaves can keep the water from reaching the roots. Other plants like tomatoes, squash, and carrots attract pests and disease more readily if their leaves get wet, so hand-watering can be one way to keep them healthy.

Hand-watering your vegetable garden can take up a lot of time, which is one definite disadvantage. It can take up to an hour to water a ten-foot-square garden and do it well. Plants often do not get enough water when they are hand-watered because gardeners rush through the task. Some gardeners enjoy this aspect of growing vegetables, as they find it relaxing, but others do not have the patience to do it. Also consider that if you hand-water your vegetables, you'll have to find someone you trust to take over for you if you want to take a vacation.

Overhead Watering

Using an overhead sprinkler is probably the easiest and most common way most gardeners water their vegetable gardens. Depending on how large your garden is, all you have to do is set up your sprinkler in one area and turn it on. Everything gets watered all at one time. It takes approximately one hour of sprinkling (depending on water pressure) for the water to soak into the soil several inches.

Benefits of Using an Overhead Sprinkler

- Simple to set up and use

- Equipment is inexpensive to purchase

- Saves time

- Timers and automatic equipment are easy to use

- Can be easily moved around your garden

- Can be used to keep plants cool in warm weather

Lettuce, spinach, salad greens, and Swiss chard all benefit from overhead watering. The leaves are kept cool while the water on the leaves evaporates, lowering the temperature of the plant and preventing plants from wilting or being scorched in hot temperatures.

Disadvantages of Using an Overhead Sprinkler

- A lot of water can be wasted through evaporation or watering areas that do not need water.

- Moisture on the leaves of some vegetable plants can cause diseases.

- Leaves of larger vegetable plants can keep moisture from reaching the plant roots.

Tomatoes, squash, and carrots do not do well if their leaves get wet. Wet leaves make these plants more susceptible to diseases such as mildew and blight. Plants with large leaves such as broccoli, cabbage, cauliflower, and corn are not good candidates for overhead watering. The leaves can prevent enough water from reaching the roots, which can cause the soil to dry out.

✳ *Smoothie Garden Solution*

One good weekly watering is much better for the plants and more effective in the soil than frequent light watering. Plant roots seek out water, and the moisture deep in the soil encourages the roots to grow deeper, which gives them access to more nutrients.

Choosing to use or not to use an overhead sprinkler is a personal choice. If time is a factor, then overhead watering may be the simplest solution. It is also important to look at the vegetables you will be growing and the effects overhead watering may have on those plants. You will have to find out which method will work best in your situation. If you have a large garden, you may be able to have the best of both worlds. You can water certain areas by hand and use overhead sprinklers for the rest.

Drip Irrigation

In drip irrigation, water seeps slowly into the soil. Gardeners use a hose that has many little holes in it or flat plastic tubing that has slits on one side. Both are laid on the ground along the base of your plants, allowing water to reach the roots. The soaker hose has the same attachments as a regular hose and is usually used in a small area where it can be easily attached to a water tap. The flat plastic tubing needs more setup to work and is common in large commercial vegetable gardens. You need irrigation connectors, attachments, and water pipe in order to attach the tubing to your water source. With good water pressure, both the soaker hose and plastic tubing can give your garden soil up to an inch of water in approximately fifteen minutes, so drip irrigation is a very efficient way to water your vegetable garden.

Advantages to Using a Drip System

- Very little water is lost to evaporation, so you don't waste water.

- Moisture reaches the roots where it is most needed.

- It adds moisture to the soil slowly, allowing it to soak in over time; this allows the roots to utilize it better.

- Soil is watered evenly and thoroughly.

- Hoses or equipment can be easily moved.

✳ *Smoothie Garden Solution*

You can recycle an old, leaky hose to make a drip irrigation system of your own! Simply punch more holes into the hose every few inches to make your own soaker hose. It's an effective way to reuse equipment you would otherwise throw into the garbage.

Make sure you have enough soaker hose or plastic tube length to cover your garden area. You can lay the hose out when you plant an area and pull it up after harvesting. For easier setup, lay it out along your beds as you plant your seeds or set out your transplants. The hose and plastic tubing can be mulched or just left on top of the ground. But be aware that both can deteriorate over time if left exposed to the sun.

Disadvantages of Drip Irrigation

- It takes time and some effort to set up and to take down the equipment and hoses.

- The tubing can be easily punctured by a rake or hoe.

- Equipment can become very costly if you have a large garden area, though it will last for a long time if handled properly.

The system using irrigation tubing is best utilized if you have a large garden or are growing commercially. It can be costly and labor-intensive, and therefore not necessarily the best choice for a small backyard vegetable garden.

Every garden site has different needs and every gardener has a different outlook, so you need to choose the watering style that best suits you and your garden. Most gardeners use a combination of all the watering options to best meet the needs of all their vegetable plants. The most important part of watering your vegetable plants is to make sure they are not getting too much or too little water. Proper watering is needed for your plants to grow and produce an abundant harvest for you.

Signs of Underwatering

A plant's roots must continually grow for the plant to stay healthy and produce its fruit, seeds, or buds. The roots draw the nutrients from the soil up into the plant to make it grow. Water allows the nutrients in the soil to be absorbed into the plant. If there is too little water, the roots cannot draw in the nutrients. As a result, the plant will not grow and mature as it should. You can water the surface or even the top several inches of your soil, but the plant roots need to go deeper into the soil to get more nutrients. This is why it is essential for regular deep watering when growing vegetables.

Wilted plants are one sign that you're not watering enough. If the plant can draw enough water to replace the amount that is evaporated from its leaves, it will remain upright and strong. If the plant is not getting the water it needs, it will quickly collapse. This causes severe stress to the plant and often death. It is important to water a plant that is wilted as soon as you can.

✳ *Smoothie Garden Solution*

Deep roots make plants more tolerant to drought conditions. If you have to ration water, know which plants have the deepest roots. Beets, asparagus, and brassicas can do with a bit less water. Never stop watering lettuce, cucumbers, and peppers, because they are very sensitive to drought conditions.

It is important to take time every day to observe your plants so you can find and quickly fix potential problems. Your plants should appear strong, have a bright color, and look healthy. If you have young transplants, you need to give them a drink of water every day because their roots are very shallow and the top few inches of your soil can dry out very quickly. Too little water can lead to poor root development, which will make for an unhealthy plant. Once your vegetable plants have begun to mature, watering them once a week is usually sufficient. For some plants, it is best to stop watering them altogether once they have matured. For example, onions and potatoes need less water as they get close to maturity.

Signs That Your Plants Need More Water

- The plants appear small and very slow-growing.

- The vegetable plants are not producing very many fruits, seeds, or buds and the ones being produced are often misshapen.

- Your plants are diseased.

- The plants are yellowish or pale in color.

- Your plants are wilting. Some natural wilting may occur in the heat of the day, but if your plants do not perk up by late afternoon you have a problem.

Signs of Overwatering

Most gardeners go to great lengths to make sure they add enough nutrients to their garden beds. When the soil is moist, the water helps hold the nutrients to rock particles in the soil so the plant roots can absorb them. If there is too much water in the soil, a process called leaching occurs. The water drains lower into the soil and takes a lot of the nutrients with it.

Vegetable plant roots grow to different depths, but most do not grow below two and a half feet. If the excess water has washed away the nutrients, there is less nourishment available for the roots to absorb. Without proper food, the plant will not grow and mature as you may expect it to.

✳ *Smoothie Garden Solution*

To make digging easier, use the heel—not the ball—of your foot to push the spade into the ground. To help prevent back strain or injury, slide the dirt off the spade or shovel rather than throwing it off.

Plants also need good air circulation to breathe. If the soil is saturated with water, there isn't any room left in the soil for air circulation. If the air supply is cut off for any length of time, the plant roots will rot, killing the plant. That's why it's crucial to know your own soil conditions. Keep a record of rainfall and regularly check the moisture in your soil either with a moisture meter or by digging into the soil with your hands or a small shovel to see how far down the moisture is. Water when needed. If you are a novice gardener, it can take time to get to know your soil and climate, so initially it is important to observe and jot down some notes so you can refer back to them the following season.

Combating Drainage Problems

You need a fertile, well-drained soil to grow great vegetables; however, most gardeners are not blessed with perfect soil or the perfect garden site.

How do you make your soil healthier and get proper drainage if you live in a rainy climate or you have soggy soil? What do you do if you have the opposite problem—a sandy soil that does not hold any amount of water? How do you increase the amount of moisture in this type of soil?

Adding organic material is the solution to both problems. It will help lighten heavy soil so the water can drain better, and it will add more organic material to the sandy soil to help hold the water in. Aged animal manure, compost, or well-drained topsoil will help. Add in as much as possible—several inches if you can get enough. It is important to add in organic matter every year because you inevitably lose soil through erosion and the process of harvesting your plants. Mulching is another way to protect your soil from being blown away or nutrients from being leached out.

✳ *Smoothie Garden Solution*

The best time to water your vegetable plants is in the morning. This gives the plant leaves time to dry off and remain cool when the sun hits. Plants—especially young seedlings—do not like to be cold, so it is best to water while the temperature is increasing during the day.

If you have an extreme problem with drainage, call a landscaper to assess the situation for you. Underground drainage pipes can help remove any excess water you may have in your garden site. A well-drained soil helps keep the plant roots from becoming waterlogged, allowing them to absorb the nutrients and oxygen needed to grow and mature. A poorly drained soil leaves your vegetable plants more susceptible to root rot and soil-borne diseases, so get help with drainage if this is a problem in your garden site.

Controlling the Weeds

A weed is just a plant that grows where it is not wanted! It is important to keep your garden beds weeded when your vegetable plants are small so your plants get a good start. Weeds compete for the nutrients in the soil, often taking over and leaving your veggie plants without the valuable food they need to grow and mature. Below you will learn different techniques to help keep your garden weed-free—or at least to help you keep the weeds under control.

Know Your Weeds

Weed seeds are introduced to your garden by birds, the wind, and on the bottom of your shoes. If a soil will not support weeds, it will not support your vegetables, so weeds are a sign that your soil is fertile. Seeds are brought to the surface by digging or tilling the soil. Once they are exposed to the light, they start growing. Some weeds can grow very fast, stealing the light, nutrients, and space from your vegetable plants.

There are three types of weeds—annuals, biennials, and perennials. Annual weeds live for only one season, but they produce thousands of seeds to ensure their survival. They germinate in the spring, produce seeds in the summer, and die in the fall. The best way to control annual weeds is to pull them out or cut them off with a hoe before they go to seed. Annual weeds grow quickly, so you need to be on top of these weeds so they do not spread their seed. Some examples of common annual weeds are knotweed, pigweed, purslane, lamb's quarters, and chickweed.

A biennial weed grows the first year but does not produce a flower or seeds until the second year of growth. The best way to control these weeds is to remove them from your garden in the first year of their growth so they have no chance of spreading their seeds. Common biennial weeds include burdock, mullein, and Queen Anne's lace.

❋ Smoothie Garden Solution

Poison ivy is the most prominent of several dangerous plants that can invade a garden, posing a threat both to your vegetables and your skin. The best way to get rid of poison ivy is to rake it out. Using a sturdy rake, carefully tug at the ivy, making sure the whole plant—including the roots—comes out. Make sure you clean your rake and wash your hands well; the oil in poison ivy can be harmful.

Perennial weeds live for years. Some produce seeds and others spread by their roots or bulbs. Perennial weeds often have deep roots that creep underground, making them difficult to eradicate. To control them, dig them out, removing as much of the root as you can. You often have to pull these weeds on a regular basis in order to get all the root system. Some common perennial weeds are dandelion, thistle, bindweed, chicory, plantain, wild sorrel, and dock.

Woody perennials include poison ivy, kudzu, morning glory, and Japanese honeysuckle. These are often invasive and are spread mainly by birds that love the seeds of these plants. Some of these plants need only a piece of stem to come in contact with soil to begin growing, so they can multiply quickly.

Grasses are another invasive perennial weed. These can make some of the worst weeds because they produce a lot of seeds and the plants are difficult to uproot. Quack grass and some varieties of bamboo are common grasses that are considered weeds, especially in the vegetable garden. These plants produce underground roots and stems, and new plants pop up several yards away from the parent plant, making them difficult to remove.

What Weeds Can Tell You

You can learn a great deal about your soil by observing the weeds that grow in your garden. They can point to soil imbalances such as poor drainage, lack of water, low fertility, lack of aeration, and nutrient deficiency. Certain weeds only grow in poor soil, which gives you an indication that you need to add more amendments and fertilize your garden area if you want to grow a successful vegetable garden. Correcting the imbalances in your soil often means you will be able to eradicate certain weeds.

Weeds That Indicate Poor Soil

- Jersey or scrub pine

- Mullein

- Oxeye daisy

- Scrub or bear oak

- Wild carrot

Weeds That Indicate Heavily Acidic Soil with Poor Drainage

- Creeping buttercup

- Docks

- Horsetail

- Thistles

- Wild sorrel

- Yarrow

Weeds That Indicate Sandy Soil

- Bindweed

- Mustards

- Ragweed

- Stinging nettles

- Wild garlic

Weeds That Indicate Inadequate Nitrogen Levels

- Clover

- Medic

- Vetch

- Wild peas

Weeds That Indicate Inadequate Essential Nutrients

- Dandelions

Weeds That Indicate Good Fertility

- Chickweed

- Chicory

- Lamb's-quarters

- Groundsel

Taking your time to observe what weeds are growing in your garden area can be especially important if you are planning to start a new garden in a certain area, or if you are looking for some property to purchase with the intention of growing your own food or growing to sell.

Weed Your Garden

As you become more familiar with your garden site and the weeds that grow there, it will get easier to distinguish weeds from your vegetable plants. As a new gardener, it can be confusing to decide what you should pull and what you should leave. Some plants look similar, especially when they are small. Lamb's-quarters looks like a radish at first and wild sorrel looks like spinach when it first starts to grow. If you aren't sure what weeds look like, delay the weeding until you see your row or the pattern of your vegetables coming up. This is another important reason to mark the area where you have planted your vegetable seeds.

❋ *Smoothie Garden Solution*

If your vegetable garden creeps onto your lawn, put in an edging between them. You can purchase plastic edging from most garden centers, or you can use wood or metal as an edging. Stone is not the best because the grass can creep in between the sections. The edging will help prevent the grass from growing into your garden site.

Getting on your hands and knees and pulling weeds (getting the roots if you can) is probably the best way to get rid of weeds in your vegetable garden. This can be time-consuming, but if you set aside time each week to do a patch, you will be pleasantly surprised to find that it can be easy to stay on top of them. Do not avoid weeding! Weeding is often a gardener's downfall because weeds can grow rapidly, and they can take over a garden before you know it. It is important to allot time every week all season long for your weeding. It is often the last thing on a gardener's list, but it should be on top. A healthy garden needs to have more veggies growing in it than weeds. If you have missed a few weeks of weeding and some of them have gone to seed, carefully pull out the plant and immediately put it into a plastic garbage bag. This will prevent some of the seeds from spreading.

Hoeing is a great way to keep the weeds in check. Get into the habit of hoeing your garden beds even if there are no weeds; this will prevent any seeds that may be in the soil from germinating. Scrape the hoe over the top inch of the soil. It is easier to hoe when the soil is moist, so do your hoeing after watering your garden or after a rainfall. By scraping the top of the soil, you will slice off the tops of the weeds, preventing the weed from going to seed. Depending on the type of weed, it may grow again or the roots may decompose. Keeping your hoe blade sharp will make this job easier to accomplish.

Mulch: Does It Work?

After hoeing or weeding your garden bed, add mulch to the area. Weed seeds need light to germinate and grow, so the main function of mulch in weed control is to prevent light from reaching the seeds. Cover the area completely with up to four inches of mulch, leaving a few inches around the base of the plant stem clear. You'll often have mulch materials handy from your own garden. Two common materials are leaves and grass. Raking leaves and then running the lawn mower over them to shred them makes great mulch. Collecting your grass clippings in a mower bag is another mulch that costs no money and is easy to get. Just make sure you do not use pesticides on your lawn; you do not want to contaminate your vegetable patch.

You can also make organic mulch out of newspaper, cardboard, straw, hay, bark mulch, compost, and animal manure. Nonorganic mulch materials include crushed rock, black plastic, and landscape fabric. These usually need to be purchased and can be expensive. Choosing the type of mulch you want to use can depend on what is readily available or how much you care about your garden's appearance. Either way, mulch is helpful in controlling the weeds in your vegetable garden.

✳ *Smoothie Garden Solution*

Tough perennial weeds will often show up when you do not have the time to deal with them. Placing boards over infested areas of quack grass, Bermuda grass, or Johnson grass will slow down their growth for a few weeks until you have the time you need to dig them out.

But mulch has many other benefits in your garden. Mulch can reduce evaporation of water so the soil will stay moist longer. It can help by either warming up the soil or keeping the temperature cool. The organic mulch will decompose over time, adding organic matter and nutrients into your garden soil. Earthworms like the darkness it provides and will thrive under a thick bed of mulch. Mulch can offer some protection to fruiting plants; it keeps their fruit from lying directly on the ground, which can help prevent pests and diseases.

However, mulch also has its disadvantages. Mulch can promote fungus and disease, especially if it keeps the soil too damp and cold. Slugs and mice love mulch, so only use mulches sparingly if you live in an area where these are a problem. Using certain types of mulch can cause deficiencies in your soil. For example, pine needles are very acidic and may make it more difficult to grow your vegetables in a soil that is already acidic. Sawdust uses up nitrogen to decompose, which it does at the expense of your plants. It is important to understand what materials are best for your garden site and the reasons you are using mulch.

Other Ways to Control Weeds

One great way to prevent weeds is not to bring them into your garden. Keep any tools you work with clean. Remove any weeds that have gone to seed from your garden. When shopping for plants, make sure there are not any weeds in the containers. When you bring in hay or straw to your garden, make sure it is from a weed-free source. If it is not weed-free, you may soon find hay growing in your garden beds! Animal manures can have lots of weed seeds in them, so make sure you know what kind of bedding was used and what the animals were fed. All of these small things can make it easier to keep your garden free of weeds, or at least ensure you are not introducing new weeds to the area.

Growing a cover crop can smother weeds. By growing a cover crop you can enrich your soil as well as control weeds. Cultivate or dig the area and then sow the green manure crop thickly. Turn the green manure over before the weeds you are trying to control have a chance to set seed. To be most effective, you will need to grow and turn two or three cover crops in succession. By growing vegetables close together, you can reduce the number of weeds by shading any area from the sun. Grow your lettuces close together so they overlap each other or grow your squash under your corn to prevent weeds from getting any light.

✳ *Smoothie Garden Solution*

Clean your gardening tools after using them. Weed seeds and diseases can be easily carried from one area to another attached to your hoe, spade, or even your shoes. Make sure you give all your tools a good rinse whenever you are finished working with them for the day to prevent infecting other areas.

Applying heat to weeds is another effective way to kill them. This is most useful in your pathways, driveway, or sidewalks. Heat will kill your vegetable plants as well, so don't use this method in your vegetable garden. You can purchase a handheld flamer, which basically burns any weeds the flame touches. To kill weeds in small areas such as the crevices of a stone patio, pour boiling water over the weeds. This will keep your patio or sidewalk weed-free.

Planting a windbreak will help prevent weeds from blowing from another area into your garden. This can be very effective, especially if your garden borders on a wooded area or a wild meadow area where there are many different weeds. You cannot usually mow or keep these areas cut back, so a windbreak keeps the seeds from reaching your garden. Cedar and laurel hedges make good windbreaks. Both grow quickly and are fairly dense when mature. A fence could also work as a windbreak, blocking unwanted seeds from coming through.

The Benefits of Weeds

Weeds do have some benefits to your garden as well. Many perennial weeds are deep-rooted, which helps bring nutrients to the surface so your vegetable plants have access to them. The deep roots also aerate the soil, which can be helpful, especially if you have drainage problems in your garden site. Weeds will grow when most other plants will not and are beneficial for preventing soil erosion and for preventing leaching of nutrients due to heavy rainfall. Many weeds are a great food source for bees, butterflies, birds, and beneficial insects, which all help to control unwanted pests and disease in your vegetable garden.

Weeds That Attract Butterflies

- Clover

- Milkweed

- Nettles

- Thistles

Weeds That Attract Songbirds

- Chickweed

- Lamb's-quarters

Weeds That Attract Beneficial Insects

- Corn spurry

- Queen Anne's lace

- Wild mustard

- White clover

Weeds can be composted so long as they have been pulled before they go to seed. If you have only pulled a few weeds, you can leave them to dry in your pathway; however, if you have a whole bucketful of weeds, it is best to remove them from the garden, because they can attract pests. Place them into your compost instead; they are a good source of green matter.

Most gardeners consider comfrey and stinging nettles to be weeds, but they can be added to your compost or used to make a nitrogen-rich fertilizer tea. Both of these plants draw up and store nitrogen in their leaves. When they are composted or made into teas, the nitrogen is released.

✳ *Smoothie Garden Solution*

Use quack grass to kill your slugs! Slugs avoid areas where this weed grows. Put some quack grass in your blender with some water to make a solution you can spray on your plants. Test the spray on a few plants; it may act too strongly on young seedlings and kill them.

There are many edible weeds that you can harvest to use in cooking. Stinging nettles, dandelion greens, purslane, lamb's-quarters, and burdock are all edible. It is important to do the research and know exactly what plant you are harvesting before you eat it. However, once you know what weeds are edible, you will have a whole new outlook and even more choices to add to your dinner table—and the weeds grew without any work on your part!

Chapter 5
Pests and Diseases

Having healthy soil and a healthy garden environment is the best way to prevent pest infestation and diseases. No garden is without pests and diseases, but the important thing is to control them before they become a problem. The secret is taking the time to observe your garden. You can keep your plants healthy and ready for use in your smoothies by using natural controls and promoting beneficial insects and pests.

Find the Problem

Take the time every day or at least once a week to walk through your garden just to observe the plants. Ignore the weeds and do not stop to harvest; just take a few minutes to turn leaves over, check inside the cabbage leaves, and look closely at any insects or pests you may see. Doing this on a regular basis will allow you to catch problems early on. Is a certain plant looking less healthy than it did last week? Are those new holes in the leaves? Is something eating my spinach? Are those cabbage flies around my brassica plants? Do my tomatoes have spots or are they split? By observing the changes to your plants you can determine whether there is a threat to the plant and act quickly.

If the problem is not obvious, you will need to be a detective to find out what could be wrong.

Questions to Ask

1. Is the problem affecting the whole plant or just part of it?

2. Is the problem on one plant or on several plants?

3. Is there a pattern to it or is the problem random?

4. Is only a certain area of the garden affected?

5. Are only young plants affected?

6. Is there anything unusual on the underside of the plant leaves?

If you can see an insect or pest but do not know what it is, try to take a sample of the problem to your local nursery to see if they can identify the problem for you. A healthy plant will be able to fight a lot of problems, so give the infected plant a little more care and attention. Does it need more or less water? Has it been fertilized recently or is it overdue? If the plant is too damaged, pull it out and immediately place it into a garbage bag and remove it from your garden site so as not to spread the problem to other areas.

✳ *Smoothie Garden Solution*

Ladybugs are a gift to any vegetable garden. They eat unwanted pests like aphids, mealybugs, spider mites, thrips, and whiteflies. To attract them to your garden, plant marigolds, goldenrod, or butterfly weed. They can also be purchased at most garden centers or from seed catalogs.

Keeping a journal of any problems you have had in your garden this season will help you to plan for next season. You can use the successes and failures as a jumping-off point for tackling problems in future seasons.

Start with Healthy Soil

Having healthy, fertile garden soil is the best way to keep pests and diseases away. First, find out what kind of soil you have and correct any imbalances. Healthy soil will produce healthy vegetable plants. Healthy vegetable plants will not be stressed and will be less vulnerable to pests or diseases. Nutrient deficiencies, overwatering, and underwatering can make your vegetable plants more susceptible to pests and diseases.

If you till your soil when it is too wet or too dry, you can harm living organisms and earthworms in the soil. You can also change the soil structure, which can cause drainage problems, leaching of nutrients, and an overall unhealthy space for your plant roots to grow. Most gardeners are raring to go in the spring and want to get the garden going, but it is important not to till too early. Take the moisture test before you till in the spring. Squeeze a handful of soil. If it forms a firm hard ball, it is too wet; if it crumbles into dust, it is too dry. Soil that is just right will keep some shape but easily crumble when you squeeze it.

✳ *Smoothie Garden Solution*

Most vegetables do best in soil with a pH between 6.0 and 6.9. Brassicas, spinach, and lettuce like it to be on the higher side. Tomatoes, peppers, eggplants, and most root crops can take the lower end. Squash, peas, beans, and onions prefer the pH to be right around 6.5.

Tilling or digging your soil in the fall will expose insects, larvae, and eggs to the elements, which can help destroy them. After you harvest an area you are going to leave bare, dig it up and let it sit for a week or so. Then either mulch the area or plant a green manure. Mulch will help keep the soil from getting too wet and will prevent leaching if you live in a rainy climate. On the flip side, mulch can also be a haven for pests such as slugs and can encourage mold and disease, so regularly check under the mulch for any larvae or eggs during the winter and spring.

Growing green manures is another way to keep your soil healthy. They are grown in the fall and help keep the soil from being blown away by the wind. Green manures also prevent erosion and leaching of nutrients. They are tilled under in the spring, which adds organic matter and nutrients to the soil, making it more fertile and healthier.

Good Gardening Practices

Maintaining a clean vegetable garden will go a long way in keeping it free of pests and disease. Trash, garden debris, and diseased plants can be a haven for many pests and diseases. Remove weeds from the garden after they are pulled out. They can be put in the compost bin or the trash if they have gone to seed. If you have any diseased vegetable plants, make sure you put them into a garbage bag immediately after pulling them so you don't spread the problem into other areas of your veggie garden.

If you find any pests, kill them on the spot by squishing them with your shoe or between your fingers. A good way to kill slugs is to cut them in half with your shovel. If you just place a pest on the ground or move it to another spot, it will be back! If you are squeamish about killing them, place them in a garbage bin and make sure they are not left on site. If the insect is too small to pick off and kill by hand, a good sharp spray of water can do the job. Spray infested leaves with an insecticidal soap or make your own insect spray to kill or deter harmful insects.

✳ *Smoothie Garden Solution*

You can buy insect sprays at your local garden center, but it's cheaper to make your own. Think of it as a smoothie for your garden's consumption. Place the following ingredients in a blender: 1 garlic bulb, 1 small onion, 1 tablespoon cayenne pepper, and 1 quart water. Blend together and let the mixture steep for a few minutes. Mix in 1 teaspoon liquid nondetergent soap. Use immediately or keep up to a week refrigerated.

When harvesting, make sure all the fruit is removed from the garden. If there are any moldy fruits, place them into the compost rather than leaving them on the ground. When a plant is matured and no longer producing, pull it out and place it into your compost. Debris that is left in your garden beds or in the pathways can easily become a home for many pests and diseases.

Always have clean, sharp tools. Take the time at the end of each day to clean your tools. Scrape off any mud or dirt from each tool and give it a good spray of water to clean it. This will remove any pests. This is especially important if you have been working with diseased plants or in an area infested by pests. Every few weeks, take a little more care and wash the blades thoroughly with soap and water, and then sharpen and oil them. A clean, sharp tool will make your life easier when working in the garden and will ensure you are not spreading pests and diseases around your garden.

✳ *Smoothie Garden Solution*

To preserve the wooden handles on your garden tools, coat them with boiled linseed oil. This type of oil is thicker and dries quicker than the edible linseed soil. Simply rub the oil into the handle, allow it to sit for five to ten minutes to penetrate the wood, and rub off any excess oil with a clean, dry cloth.

Crop rotation is another essential practice to ensure a healthy garden. By growing your veggie plants in a different area each year, you will discourage pests and diseases in your soil. Each vegetable plant or family of plants requires different nutrients and attracts different pests and diseases. These pests usually live in the soil right where the plant was, so by moving your plants to a new area of the garden they will be less likely to survive. A good rule of thumb is not to plant the same vegetable or family of vegetables in the same area for four years.

Companion planting is another practice that can help to keep pests and diseases away from certain plants. In this method, certain plants are grown together so that they help each other. One plant may attract beneficial insects that will eat common pests, keeping the plants nearby healthier. Another plant may deter a pest, keeping the plant beside it healthier.

Keep Your Plants Healthy

To have healthy vegetable plants, you need to start with healthy seeds and transplants. Buy your seeds from a reputable seller or—even better—save your own seeds, especially if you find a certain variety that does well in your garden! A reputable seller should be willing to answer all your questions, provide you with information on where and how the seeds were grown, and give you growing tips. If your garden site is susceptible to certain pests or diseases, try to find seed varieties that are resistant to the problem. Seed catalogs have valuable information regarding different varieties of seeds. Choosing the right varieties of vegetable plants for your garden will help to keep the soil and plants healthier.

When you purchase plants or transplants, make sure they are healthy. Many gardeners have unknowingly brought pests and diseases into their gardens via transplants. Look closely at any transplants you are planning to bring home. Check for any insects in the soil or on the undersides of the leaves, holes in the leaves, and evidence that insects have chewed the leaves. These are all signs that the plant may be infested. Make sure the plant looks healthy. The stem should be strong and thick, the leaves should be well formed and a bright green color, and the plant should not be root-bound.

✳ *Smoothie Garden Solution*

To quickly transplant your seedlings, use a bulb planter to make the holes. The hole is just the right size for individual plastic cells. Gently drop each seedling into the hole and cover it with the soil you pulled out. Firm the soil around the base of the plant.

When you set out your transplants or weed around them, make sure you do not damage the plant roots. Injured roots are more likely to attract pests and diseases, and a stressed or damaged plant will be less likely to fight off problems.

When planning your garden layout, make sure you calculate how many plants you will need. Most gardeners purchase too many and then think they have to squeeze all the plants into their garden. Plants need a certain amount of space to grow well, so be careful not to overcrowd them. Vegetable plants will grow better with good air circulation, which will help prevent mold or fungus on the leaves or fruit. Keeping fruit off the ground will also keep the plant and fruit healthier; if the fruit is touching the wet soil, it will often rot before it is harvested.

Correct watering is another important aspect to keeping your plants healthy. Most vegetable plants need at least one inch of water each week, although this will vary depending on the specific plant and your climate, rainfall, and soil conditions. Plants that get either too much or too little water will be more likely to attract pests and diseases.

Regularly fertilizing your vegetable plants will help keep them healthier as well. Record how much and when you fertilize them so you don't give them too much or too little.

Use Natural Controls

Okay, you have kept your garden clean, your tools clean, and you have tried to keep your plants healthier, but you still have some pest and disease problems. Do not fret—a few problems don't mean you have to throw it all in and quit. There are some easy ways to control any problems you may have. It is important to observe your garden on a regular basis so you can catch any potential problems early on; problems are much easier to handle if not too many plants are infected.

Larger pests or animals can cause a lot of damage in vegetable gardens. Deer, elk, raccoons, squirrels, opossum, skunks, gophers, and bears like vegetables just as much as we do. Take the time to observe what kind of animal is entering your garden. They often come out and feed at dusk or dawn. If it's not a wild animal, maybe your neighbor's dog or cat is sneaking in and digging up your plants. Keep watch to see what is causing the problem.

If you need to set physical traps to stop insects and other animals, consider the following:

- Set mice traps.

- Put out a dish of beer to attract slugs or lay a board for them to crawl under and then destroy them.

- Use cutworm collars around the base of the plant to prevent the cutworm from climbing up the stem.

- Set out sticky yellow flytraps, which will attract the flea beetle. The flea beetle sticks to the trap and dies.

- Use row covers to prevent flea beetles, carrot rust flies, or cabbage flies from reaching the veggie plants so they can't lay their eggs on them.

- Build a fence to keep out dogs, cats, raccoons, bear, and deer.

Attracting predators that will eat your pests is another natural way to keep the cycle in your garden healthy. Grow flowers, herbs, and certain vegetable plants to attract birds, ladybugs, honeybees, and lacewings, which will keep a lot of your pest problems under control.

Harmful Pests Versus Beneficial Insects and Animals

When you first begin to garden, there is a lot to learn about which bugs are good for your garden and which ones are harmful. It takes time to get to know what is living in or entering your garden, and each year may bring a new problem. Learn by asking fellow gardeners, reading books, checking out the Internet, or ask questions at your local nursery or garden center. Vegetable gardening is a new experience each season because you cannot predict what will happen. Do not be afraid to experiment with new plant varieties and try out different natural controls. Stay away from pesticides when it comes to your vegetable garden; they will not make your soil healthier and will kill the beneficial insects as well as the pests. Attracting and keeping beneficial animals and insects in your garden brings you closer to having healthier plants and a more abundant vegetable harvest.

Birds, bats, toads, and snakes are all animals you want in your garden. They will keep the slugs, snails, and many insects under control. All these animals need food, water, and shelter. Your unwanted pests give them all the food they need, but you may need to supply water and shelter for these animals in order for them to stick around. If you do not have an existing water pond or fountain, place some water bowls around your garden and keep them filled. Place a birdhouse in a tree near your garden. A bat house looks like a flattened birdhouse with a thin slot for the entrance; they can also be kept in trees. Use a clay flowerpot with a chipped rim as a toad house. Place the pot upside down near a water source. Snakes will live in a pile of rocks or a pile of sticks; just leave a bit of space in between for them to crawl into. Making a home for these animals will help control the ones you do not want!

✳ Smoothie Garden Solution

Birds will keep harmful insects under control but will also eat your corn seedlings and strawberries. If the birds are eating the seeds, cover your seedbeds with bird netting until the seeds have sprouted. Some gardeners tie colored tape to tree branches and fences, which can be effective in keeping the birds out of your garden.

There are as many beneficial insects as there are harmful ones. Each garden site has a variety of different insects and soil animals.

Common Beneficial Insects

- Earthworms
- Ground beetles
- Honeybees
- Lacewings
- Ladybugs
- Praying mantises
- Spiders
- Syrphid flies

- Tachina flies

- Wasps

- Yellow jackets

Planting flowers among your vegetables or letting some of your vegetable plants flower rather than pulling out the plant is another way to attract beneficial insects to your garden. The flowers add color to your garden, some are edible, and they can make your garden more attractive overall.

Flowers That Attract Beneficial Insects

- Broccoli flowers

- Calendula

- California poppy

- Celery flowers

- Dill flowers

- Lemon balm

- Marigolds

- Nasturtiums

- Parsley flowers

- Sunflowers

Having a healthy ecosystem in your vegetable garden lets nature take care of things for you. Start with healthy soil, plant healthy seeds and plants, and create an environment that will keep everything in your garden in balance.

Common Diseases

You can physically see a pest or insect, but it is more difficult to diagnose a plant disease because the symptoms can be similar to those caused by other factors like excessive heat or cold, nutrient deficiencies in the soil, or poor drainage. Having healthy soil, giving your plants proper water and fertilizer, and maintaining good garden practices minimizes your plants' vulnerability to many diseases. If you do have a recurring problem, it is important to learn what it is and try to correct the cause.

There are four main types of pathogens that cause disease in vegetable plants—bacteria, fungi, nematodes, and viruses. They all attack plants in different ways but have some common symptoms such as wilting, yellowing, and stunted growth. The pathogens can be spread in various ways. They can be blown around by the wind or carried in water. Animals, humans, garden tools, and other equipment can also transfer them from plant to plant. Insects can carry a pathogen in their saliva and transfer it from plant to plant. When you are trying to diagnosis a disease, it is important to learn the life cycle of the pathogen so you can avoid spreading it.

✳ *Smoothie Garden Solution*

Aphids can easily spread viral and bacterial diseases. Controlling aphids often helps you stop the spread of the disease. Control aphids by attracting braconid wasps, hoverflies, lacewings, and ladybugs to your garden. An alternative is knocking the aphids off the plant with a strong stream of water.

Before any disease can occur, three elements must be present in your garden: a susceptible plant, a pathogen, and favorable conditions for the pathogen to survive. To control or manage plant diseases, you need to remove one or more of these elements. A disease cannot develop if one of these elements is missing. Planting disease-resistant varieties of vegetables can remove a susceptible plant from this equation. Pulling out and destroying the infected vegetable plant removes the pathogen. You can make it difficult for pathogens to survive by creating an environment that is not compatible for them. For example, avoid overhead watering or take time to trellis a plant so it has better air circulation. Both of these measures make it more difficult for the pathogen to survive.

The best way to keep your vegetable garden free of pests and diseases is to have healthy soil, to give your plants the proper amount of water, to use crop rotation, and to keep your garden and tools clean. A healthy plant will be better able to fight off anything that comes its way. No vegetable garden will be totally free of all pests or diseases, and remember that you want beneficial insects and animals to stay around.

Chapter 6
Greenhouse Gardening

If you have a wet garden site, want to extend your growing season, or prefer not to work in unpredictable outdoor weather, you can grow your vegetable garden in a greenhouse. Indoor gardening is also a great complement to growing outdoors because you can give your vegetable plants the head start or extra protection they may need. In this chapter, you will learn about the advantages to growing your vegetables indoors and the various structures that can be used for growing. It also means you'll have fresh veggies all year round for your smoothies.

Extend Your Growing Season

Most gardeners would love to grow and eat their own fresh vegetables all year round, but most do not live in a climate where this is possible. Growing in a cold frame, plastic tunnel, or greenhouse are ways to start plants earlier in the spring and grow through the cooler and rainy fall months—and possibly during the cold winters. If you live in a climate that has a short growing season (early June to late August, for example), starting your seedlings indoors in early spring is necessary if you want to have a productive garden. Otherwise, vegetable plants such as tomatoes, peppers, and squash will not have enough warm days to mature if planted by seed.

For gardeners who want to have an early spring harvest of salad greens or baby carrots, growing indoors is a great place to start. Unpredictable weather during late winter and early spring can make outdoor planting nearly impossible. If you live in a hot climate, it's important to start vegetables such as spinach and brassicas early enough so they can be well established before the summer heat arrives. They need be started in early spring when the weather is not cooperating, so starting your seedlings indoors is the answer.

✳ *Smoothie Garden Solution*

Humans have used the phases of the moon as a guide to identify the best times for planting since ancient times. According to this method, plant above-ground vegetables when the moon is increasing (waxing) and below-ground vegetables when the moon is decreasing (waning). The Old Farmer's Almanac website (*www.almanac.com*) and the gardening advice at *www.your-vegetable-gardening-helper.com* both have great information on the subject.

For harvesting vegetables in the fall and winter, plants usually need to be started in July. Cold or rainy weather often hits before they can mature, so growing them indoors is one solution. Another way to extend your growing season is to place a heater in your greenhouse, giving your veggies the extra warmth they need to grow and be harvested during the cooler fall and winter months. Start seedlings and grow through the shorter days of winter using a grow lamp or lights. This can give your vegetable plants that little extra light they need to do well.

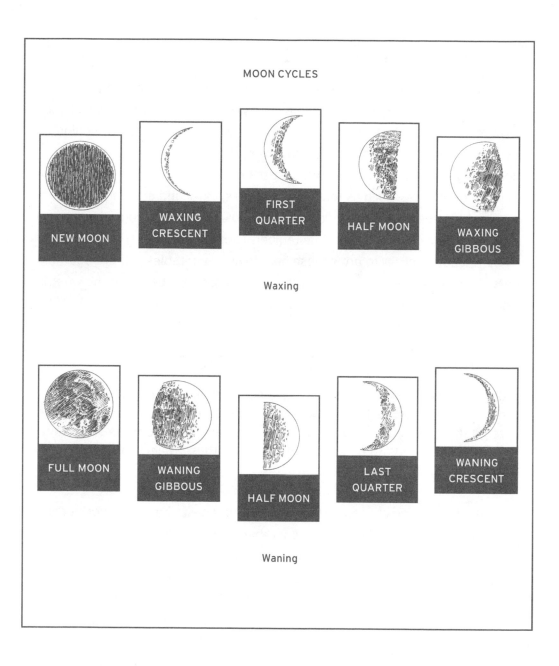

MOON CYCLES

NEW MOON · WAXING CRESCENT · FIRST QUARTER · HALF MOON · WAXING GIBBOUS

Waxing

FULL MOON · WANING GIBBOUS · HALF MOON · LAST QUARTER · WANING CRESCENT

Waning

Protect Your Plants

By growing your vegetables indoors, you'll have more control over the amount of heat, light, and water your vegetable plants get. You can add artificial light, control heat, and control your plants' access to water. In contrast, when you grow your vegetables outdoors, you have very little—if any—control over how much sunlight or rainfall your vegetable beds get.

Some vegetables, such as tomatoes, peppers, okra, and eggplants, need extra heat to grow their best. If you live in a cooler climate or your garden site is at a higher elevation with extreme temperature fluctuations, a greenhouse may be needed in order to grow these heat-loving vegetables. Other vegetable plants such as lettuce, spinach, and salad greens grow better when the weather is cooler and may need protection if the weather gets too hot.

✳ *Smoothie Garden Solution*

Corn, trellised peas, and climbing beans are all great sun screeners for other vegetables. As they grow they will give smaller and more tender vegetable plants the shade and protection they need from the sun. Plant your lettuces and other salad greens around these taller plants during the hot summer months.

Tomatoes and carrots can attract diseases and pests if their leaves become damp. It is very beneficial for these vegetable plants to be grown under cover where you can control how they are watered. Drip irrigation is often used in greenhouse settings and is a very effective way of watering your vegetables.

Growing indoors can help you prevent certain pests and diseases from reaching your vegetable plants. For example, flea beetles can devastate a bed of Oriental or salad greens. These little black beetles eat holes in the leaves and stunt the plants' growth. If your garden is susceptible to this pest, you have more control over it if you grow the affected crops indoors or under cover where the insect cannot reach them. Growing indoors can also prevent blight from ruining your tomato crop. Blight is caused by a fungus that spreads rapidly if the tomato plant's leaves get wet, especially during late July and early August.

Cold Frames

Cold frames work by capturing sunlight during the day and holding the heat inside through the night. There is no one standard size for cold frames, but the back is usually higher than the front, giving them a slanted top. They are usually built facing south in order to capture as much sunlight as possible. You want to position your cold frame in a sunny spot against a house, shed, or hillside for added protection from the wind. These structures are mainly used for overwintering tender plants and for growing trays of seedlings in the spring. It can also be used as a raised bed in the summer months if you simply leave the lid open or remove it altogether.

If you have access to an electric outlet, a cold frame can become a hothouse. You can bury an electric cable in the dirt or sand and then place trays of seedlings on top of the sand, allowing the seedling trays to be heated from the bottom. Some vegetable seedlings such as tomatoes, peppers, and squash need a high, consistent temperature to germinate and this type of hothouse is the perfect way to start them.

✳ *Smoothie Garden Solution*

Winter gardening means planting vegetables in the summer and then harvesting during the winter. These plants usually reach maturity by the end of October and are eaten throughout the winter. *Overwintering* means planting certain vegetables in late summer or early fall and harvesting them the following spring.

Plywood, cement, and stone bricks are the most common materials used in making cold frames. The roofing material is usually a clear product such as glass, plastic, or fiberglass. Old window frames or glass doors can be recycled to construct the roof. The bottom of the cold frame may be left uncovered or may have a variety of bottom coverings depending on what you use it for. If you are growing winter crops, you want to have a fertile, well-drained soil with amendments added every year. If you are using it for overwintering containers or starting seedlings, consider a floor of bricks, because they will retain heat longer and help maintain a consistent temperature in the structure. If you are making a hothouse for your heat-loving seedlings, you will want to bury your electric heating cable and cover it with an inch of sand. This will keep the bottom of the seedlings at the same temperature, which is what they need to germinate well.

Planning how you want to use your cold frame will help you determine your design and the materials you need to build it. A cold frame can be an inexpensive structure made from recycled or common materials that you have on hand or can easily get. It is easy to construct and can be used in a variety of ways all season long.

Plastic Tunnels

These structures are made of plastic or metal hoops with plastic sheeting secured over the hoops. Sizes vary depending on your needs. Your tunnel can be large enough to walk through or just the right size to protect your vegetables.

The plastic tunnel is used in much the same way as the cold frame, just on a larger scale. It is used to give young seedlings the protection they need in early spring, to grow heat-loving vegetables in the summer, and to grow winter crops for harvesting in the fall. It is usually unheated. It is not necessarily a permanent structure; in fact, it can be easily moved to different areas of your garden each season as you rotate your crops.

✳ *Smoothie Garden Solution*

Why should you rotate your vegetables? First, rotating vegetables within the same family will help prevent disease and insect damage to your garden. Second, different vegetables use different amounts of nutrients. By moving them to a different area each year, you help prevent the depletion of the essential nutrients in your garden soil.

The plastic tunnel is less expensive to construct than a glass greenhouse and can be just as effective. Plastic tunnels are often easier to vent than glass ones since the plastic is usually moveable. Some are even constructed to allow you to manually roll up the bottom sides, letting the cool air in and the excess heat out. You have to be aware that by opening the sides or ends you are also allowing pests to reach your veggie plants, so it is important to plan what you will be growing and why and vent accordingly.

Plastic tunnel

One concern with the tunnels is that they can become too warm inside during the hot summer months. Too much heat can damage your plants just as much as too much cold, so it is important to have a way to ventilate your structure. You do not want your tunnel to get too much above 90°F for any length of time without allowing cool air in and excess hot air out. It is important to have a thermometer inside the tunnel at all times to monitor the temperature.

Construct Your Own Plastic Tunnel

1. Decide the length and width you want your tunnel to be. Most tunnels are about 2-3 feet wide. It is best to space your hoops 3-5 feet apart so your structure is sturdy.

2. Choose a lightweight material if you are planning to move your tunnel. Try a plastic water pipe—½"-¾" in diameter works well for the hoops. The pipes can be purchased in various lengths and bend easily. Many seed catalogs have cloche pipe, which you can also use to construct your tunnel.

3. Sink two 2-foot lengths of rebar or a metal stake at least one foot into the ground. Place the plastic pipe over the exposed length; this will help to keep the hoops in place.

4. Use greenhouse plastic to cover the frame you have constructed. Make sure you purchase an extra two feet of plastic so you can easily secure it to the end hoops.

5. Use garden clips to attach the plastic to the hoops. These anchor the plastic and can be purchased in many seed catalogs.

6. Drape plastic over each end and secure it with your clips. The ends can also be left open for ventilation; the decision will depend on what you want to use your tunnel for and what time of year it is.

Keep the plastic clear of snow and other objects that may weigh it down. Place a thermometer in the center of the tunnel so you can keep an eye on the temperature. A plastic tunnel with open ends usually has enough ventilation for a 10- to 20-foot tunnel. Anything longer may need additional ventilation on the sides, especially if you get hot weather during the summer months. The easiest way to ventilate the sides of your plastic tunnel is to lift the plastic from the ground and place a box or crate under it, leaving an open space on either side of the crate. Do this every ten feet on either side of the tunnel; this will allow cool air in and push the warmer air out the ends.

Glass Greenhouses

The glass greenhouse is a permanent and more expensive structure for your garden. It serves the same functions as a cold frame or plastic tunnel. The glass greenhouse is usually more attractive to look at and can be built to suit your garden style. Greenhouses come in all sizes and prices. If you are choosing to build a glass greenhouse, make sure you shop around and choose a quality product. They are often complicated and heavy to construct, so see if the price includes installation. Since greenhouses are permanent structures, it may be expensive to build one. Be sure you know what you are going to use it for and get one that works best for your needs.

Glass lasts longer than plastic, giving a greenhouse a clear advantage over cold frames and plastic tunnels. Plastic can easily be torn or punctured and has a life span of three to four years at the most. A properly installed and maintained glass greenhouse can last several decades. Plastic tunnels are often said to be easier to ventilate, but a glass greenhouse can be equipped with vents that automatically open and close when the inside temperature reaches a preset number. This means you don't have to do all the dirty work of checking the temperature and setting up manual vents yourself.

Some greenhouses are made of fiberglass rather than glass. Fiberglass is a strong yet lightweight manmade product that can easily be cut into shapes to fit your needs. It can be more desirable than glass because it lasts even longer, but it is often more expensive and can become scratched if it is not kept clean.

✳ *Smoothie Garden Solution*

Amending and fertilizing your soil with manure is just as important in an indoor vegetable garden as it is for your outside garden beds. Bird and bat guano are the animal manures with the highest nitrogen content. The next highest are rabbit, poultry, and sheep manures. The animal manures with the least nitrogen are cow, pig, and horse.

It's easier to add artificial heat and light to a permanent greenhouse structure than to a plastic tunnel. This allows you to extend your harvest, giving you fresh veggies all year long. However, a permanent structure may need more maintenance and can be more costly to repair than a cold frame or plastic tunnel.

Greenhouse Maintenance

When growing your vegetables indoors, it is important to have a balance of water, ventilation, and heat for your plants to grow well. It is best to water your plants from below and you must be careful not to overwater them. Temperatures can change drastically from day to night, so checking the temperature often will help you make decisions on when to ventilate or whether to add heat. Ventilation during the bright, sunny days is extremely important to maintain the temperature throughout the day and night. If you have automatic vents, make sure they are checked regularly and serviced if needed. Having a thermometer is essential in your cold frame, plastic tunnel, or greenhouse.

Keeping your greenhouse free of debris will help prevent disease and pests. Make sure to remove weeds from the structure. If you are removing diseased plants, make sure you place them into a plastic bag as soon as you pull them out or cut them so as not to spread the problem to other plants or your soil.

Fall or early spring are ideal times to wash and clean the glass in your greenhouse and the lid of your cold frame. A clean surface will allow more sunlight to reach your plants, so take the time to wash the glass inside and out. It is also important to clean and disinfect any shelving or tables you may have in your greenhouse to discourage the spread of disease. Organizing any items you may have stored and removing all old plants and debris will discourage pests from finding a home. Repair or replace anything that may be broken or in need of attention.

If you have a plastic tunnel, keep the plastic clean by sweeping off any debris and giving the outside a good spray with your hose. Look for tears or holes in the plastic. You can cover small tears with tape, but if you see larger tears or several holes it is best to replace the plastic altogether. Make sure the hoops and plastic are secure; if you live in a windy area, bury the plastic along the sides to make the structure more secure. If you will not be growing or using the tunnel over the winter, take it down and store the material. The materials will definitely last longer this way.

✳ *Smoothie Garden Solution*

Once you have pulled out harvested plants, sow a cover crop in their place. Once the cover crop has grown a few inches tall, till the crop under or pull it out and place it into your compost. Either way increases the organic matter in your soil.

A healthy, nutrient-rich soil is important for growing great-tasting vegetables. Amending your soil by adding in organic matter in the spring and fall will help keep your soil rich. Fertilizing with the three essential nutrients—nitrogen, phosphorus, and potassium—is also very important, so do a soil test every few years to give yourself an indication of what your soil may need. Knowing the pH level of your soil will help in planning what you want to grow and whether you need to increase or decrease the number.

Best Veggies for the Greenhouse

All vegetables can be grown indoors given the right conditions. Vegetable plants that are grown indoors need the same conditions as they do outdoors. They need fertile soil, the right amount of sun, and proper watering, fertilizing, and care. Some vegetables will do better indoors because the heat and moisture can be regulated. Just because plants are grown indoors does not mean they will grow or mature more quickly.

The best vegetables to grow indoors in the early spring include the following:

- Carrots

- Lettuce

- Radishes

- Salad greens

- Spinach

- Swiss chard

The heat of the summer months helps vegetables mature, but growing the following vegetables indoors gives them the extra heat they may need, especially if you live in a cooler climate:

- Beans

- Cucumbers

- Eggplant

- Okra

- Oriental vegetables

- Peppers

- Tomatoes

Fall brings cooler nights and often wetter weather, so planting some vegetables indoors protects them from excess water, lower temperatures, and snow. The best vegetables for growing indoors during the fall months include the following:

- Beets

- Carrots

- Lettuce

- Scallions

- Spinach

If you want to get a head start with your vegetable garden, starting your own seedlings can be very satisfying and easier on your pocketbook than purchasing them from your local garden store. The best plants to start as seedlings include the following:

- Brassicas

- Eggplants

- Onions

- Peppers

- Tomatoes

Growing your vegetables indoors in a cold frame, plastic tunnel, glass greenhouse, or a combination of any of these methods will allow you to extend your growing season. Any of these structures would be a great enhancement to your vegetable growing and your backyard.

Chapter 7
Top Gardening Tools

Planting and tending your vegetable garden is easier and a lot more fun if you are working with the right tools for the job. If you are a novice gardener, you will only need some basic tools that are usually fairly inexpensive and easy to find. This chapter details the top garden tools, tips on how to choose them, the importance of keeping your tools clean, and methods for sharpening them.

Choosing the Right Tool

In vegetable gardening, there are some basic tasks that require some basic tools. Vegetable gardening is definitely a hands-on activity, so prepare to get your hands dirty! The basic tasks start in the spring with digging the garden beds, getting them ready for planting, moving amendments and debris to and from the garden site, planting the seeds for transplants, watering, harvesting, and making compost.

Basic gardening tools can be purchased at garden centers, hardware stores, and garage sales or flea markets. If you purchase them secondhand, just make sure they are in good shape. Try to set a budget when purchasing tools; they can vary in price. Always choose the best quality you can afford! Blades should be forged from a single piece of metal and should have a solid socket construction where they meet the handle. Studies have shown that a D-shaped handle is easiest to use. Choose a handle made of wood, metal, or good quality plastic for the best longevity of the tool.

✳ *Smoothie Garden Solution*

Proper footwear is important in the garden, especially if you will be doing any digging. A boot with a heavy sole will make it easier to press down on a spade or shovel when digging or moving amendments or compost. If your garden is uneven, proper footwear can prevent you from tripping or falling.

When you go looking for your vegetable gardening tools, make sure you purchase the right tools for you. Choose the size and weight that will work best for you. You want to be able to dig, hoe, or rake without straining your back or arms. Someone who is five feet tall will need a different size tool than a person who is six feet tall in order to use it properly and with ease. Choose a handle that works for your height and make sure the circumference of the handle fits comfortably in your hand.

Shovels

You'll need a shovel for making, digging, or tilling your garden beds. There are two basic shovels—round edged and flat edged. Each has different functions, but you may only need one depending on what kind of garden site you have. A round-edged shovel is used for scooping and lifting soil. This type of shovel is great for turning your garden beds and adding in organic amendments such as compost or aged animal manure. A shovel with a flat rectangular blade is used more for prepping a garden bed. They work well for cutting edges, stripping sod, digging holes, and prying up rocks.

Choose a shovel with a smooth, rounded shoulder at the top of the blade to protect your feet when pressing down on the shovel. When using the shovel, stand up straight while digging and bend your knees when lifting. When moving material from one area to another, turn your whole body, not just your hips. This will help protect you from any back strains or injuries.

Garden Fork

You'll need two different garden forks. One is used for digging and the other for turning your compost. The digging fork (sometimes called a spading fork) is used for turning over soil, mixing in soil amendments, lifting and breaking up clumps of soil, and harvesting root crops. The compost fork (sometimes called a pitchfork) is ideal for turning and moving compost, mulches, straw, green manures, and other organic material used in or around your garden beds.

✳ *Smoothie Garden Solution*

Your computer can be a useful tool for gardening. Set up a garden chart on your computer and update it regularly with information regarding when, where, and what you planted. Keep track of how each plant did and how much you harvested. This will be a great resource to look back on when planning for next season.

Your digging fork should have four broad, flat metal tines with V-shaped ends. You want a solid fork with a bit of weight to it so that you can easily turn soil or lift out rocks without the tines bending. The compost fork has four fine, curved tines that can easily penetrate and hold on to the organic matter. You want this fork to be lighter because you will be doing more lifting and throwing of materials with it.

When choosing a fork, make sure the size and weight are a good fit for you. Always choose the best quality you can afford.

Rake

The rake is used for preparing and cleaning your garden bed and for collecting organic matter like garden debris and leaves. You want a garden rake that has a long handle attached to a bar with small tines. This type of rake is used for leveling and cleaning any larger pebbles and debris from your planting bed. A fine clean bed is necessary when planting seeds like carrots, radishes, turnips, rutabagas, and salad greens.

The garden rake can be used for raking up leaves, grass clippings, and other garden debris, but a leaf rake is much easier to work with for these jobs. The leaf rake or landscape rake has longer teeth that are arranged in a fan style. The tines or teeth are usually made of steel, plastic, or bamboo. This allows you to easily rake up a larger amount of debris.

✳ *Smoothie Garden Solution*

You've seen the slapstick comedy bit where someone steps on a rake and it swings upward and hits the person in the face. This can look funny in a movie, but it can cause serious injury to a person if it happens in your garden. Be aware of where you leave your rake and never leave it with the tines facing upward!

When choosing a rake, make sure it fits your body. You want to be able to stand upright while raking so you don't injure or strain your back. If the rake is too long or too short, it will be difficult to work with.

Hoe

The hoe is used to dig up persistent and stubborn weeds. There are several different types of hoes you can purchase depending on your needs. The basic one is a gooseneck hoe, which has a flat edge that is used for digging and chopping weeds. The stirrup hoe is easier to use when weeding your garden beds because it slices the top inch or so of the soil, cutting the weeds off just below the soil surface. This motion is easier on your back and shoulders than the digging motion you make with the gooseneck hoe.

The handle of the hoe should be forty-eight to fifty-four inches long. This is a good length for working standing upright. Keep the blade sharp and slide it parallel to the soil to loosen the weeds and sever the roots. Hoe in the evening just before the sun goes down to discourage the weeds from germinating. It is easier to hoe when the soil is moist, but if it has been dry, hoeing hard soil will help it to absorb the moisture better when it does rain.

Trowel

The hand trowel is handy for digging a hole when setting out your transplants or planting garlic bulbs or seed potatoes. A hoe will do a similar job, but a trowel is easier to work with because you are generally close to the ground when you are planting your vegetables. You can also use the trowel as a measuring stick. You can purchase some trowels with the depth measurements written on the blade or you can make your own marks on one you already have. Having a measurement marker makes it easier to get the correct depth when planting your seeds, bulbs, or seed potatoes.

✳ *Smoothie Garden Solution*

Reuse some items around your home as tool holders. Old golf bags can be used as carts. Aprons with large pockets, wicker or plastic baskets, backpacks, and wagons can be also be used to hold items. Using a holder will make it easier to keep all the tools you need in one place.

Using the trowel and hoe together is a great way to make a straight garden row to place your seeds. Use the handle of your hoe as a marker for the row and then use the trowel to make a trench to the desired depth.

Wheelbarrow

The wheelbarrow is an essential tool for the vegetable gardener. It is used for hauling items to and from your garden site. The wheelbarrow can be used for transporting large amounts of harvested vegetables and carrying large amounts of plant material to your compost area. You can hang your garlic or onions over the sides of the wheelbarrow and use it to easily move them in and out of the sun.

There are many different types of wheelbarrows. The most common has a single wheel with two handles for pushing. Before choosing a wheelbarrow, make sure you know what you will be using it for and how much weight you will be hauling in it. If you are going to be carrying heavy loads, then choosing a sturdy metal one is probably best. If you have a small garden and will only use the wheelbarrow for lighter loads, then a lightweight plastic or cloth type may work better for you. When purchasing a wheelbarrow, take the time to push it around in the store. If it feels heavy for you when it is empty, go for a model that is more lightweight. It will only get heavier when you fill it up!

Garden Hose

No matter how small your garden is, you will be less likely to water your plants adequately if you have to pack water. Make sure you have a water source nearby. Your garden hose should be able to reach the far end of your garden. Hoses come in different lengths and can be easily connected together to make a length that works for your garden site.

Hoses come in a variety of styles and are usually a half inch to one inch in diameter. The bigger the hose diameter, the faster the water will come through, although this may vary depending on your water pressure. Choose a no-kink hose so you can easily move it around without it twisting and disrupting your water flow. Purchase the best quality hose you can afford. You can spend a lot of money on hose carriers and systems to roll them up; what you choose will depend on your garden site.

✳ *Smoothie Garden Solution*

Make up a transplanting kit with some tools from your house. Your kit should include small scissors for thinning seedlings, a teaspoon to move a tiny transplant from one pot to another, a wooden spoon for making holes for seedlings, tweezers for picking up tiny seeds, and a salt shaker for sowing tiny seeds.

Attaching a water wand or nozzle to the end of your hose can make gardening easier as well. Water wands allow you to reach the plant more easily and without straining. Buy a nozzle that has several spray options so you can water your vegetable plants in different ways.

Sharp Knife

A small sharp kitchen knife is one of the most flexible tools a home gardener can have. A simple paring knife is great for opening bags of fertilizer, cutting string, harvesting vegetables, cutting off stems of plants for composting, cutting off diseased or pest-infected plants, and slicing into a tomato or cucumber to eat it! Buy one just for your garden tool kit.

Garden Gloves

Working in soil or with other organic materials can give your hands a beating. Digging or shoveling for any length of time is a sure way to give yourself a blister if you are doing it with bare hands. Weeding can be hard on the fingernails and fingertips. A good pair of gloves will help to protect your hands from all these.

Make sure the gloves you choose fit snugly but aren't too tight. If they are too large, they will fall off every time you set a tool down. Large gloves also make it harder to grip anything. Choose a pair of gloves that fits well and is made with a breathable material. Buy a couple of pairs so you'll always have a spare when one pair is in the wash. If you are working in wet soil, rubber kitchen gloves are a good option for keeping your hands dry.

Garden Journal

Keeping track of information such as where you planted certain vegetables, how they grew, and what gardening methods worked or did not work is invaluable for planning and troubleshooting in future seasons. The journal can be as fancy or as simple as you want it to be. Choosing a book with some kind of binding or folder is best. Scraps of paper can be easily misplaced and are harder to look back on.

There are several types of garden journals, and all have valuable tips and information for the vegetable gardener. Making your own can save you money and allows you to customize your journal according to what you want and need.

The following are important notations you should always include in your journal:

- A drawing or map of your garden site

- A section for each type of vegetable (or family of vegetable) (List the variety you planted, where it was planted, and the maturity date. As the season progresses, jot down how well it grew, whether your harvest was successful, and whether you would grow this variety again.)

- A place to note when you fertilized each vegetable, with what, how much, and the results

- A section for maintenance notes (This is where you will detail any pest or disease problems, your remedies, and their results.)

Writing in a garden journal is one of the best habits a vegetable gardener can have. You'll forget the details of your gardening experience by the time next season rolls around, but if you keep a journal you'll be able to look back. Even little notes about the weather and how many birds or butterflies were in your garden each season are interesting to review. It is important to jot down your thoughts about what worked or did not work to make it easier to plan for next season.

Cleaning and Sharpening Your Tools

It is extremely important to clean your tools, pots, and work surfaces, especially when they have come into contact with diseased plants or soil. If you do not take the time to clean them the disease can easily and quickly spread throughout your whole garden. Even if you are not working with diseased plants, it is still a good practice to clean your tools on a regular basis. Every gardener should get into the habit of cleaning off any dirt and wiping the tool after every use.

After working in your garden, remove the tools from the garden area and scrape the soil off them. Wipe the tool clean and store it in its proper place. Brush or sweep all benches or surfaces. Clean pots or pails with a solution of one part bleach to ten parts water.

✳ *Smoothie Garden Solution*

Having a large, well-organized garden shed is a luxury most gardeners do not have, but it is important to organize your tools and equipment in the storage space you do have. Keep frequently used items where you can easily reach them. If you have an organized space, you will be less likely to purchase duplicate tools, which will save you money!

Do a thorough cleaning of all your tools at the end of the season before you put them away into storage. Rub off any debris with a cloth or burlap sack. If the dirt is dried on, use a wire brush or steel wool to scrape it all off. Then wipe any metal parts lightly with oil (car oil works well) and wipe wooden handles with boiled linseed oil. A good quality tool that is properly used and cared for can last you several decades.

Having a sharp tool will make gardening tasks easier to accomplish. All tools should be regularly sharpened, but pay particular attention to your hoe and digging tools. These should be sharpened before you start to work in the garden. When hoeing your beds, you may need to sharpen the hoe blade in the middle of the project, especially if you are working in a large area.

To sharpen your tools, smoothly draw a flat file down the blade from top to bottom. Do not go back and forth; just move the file in one direction. File the blade until all the nicks are smoothed out. When the blade is sharp to the touch, move the file over the back edge of the tool to remove any buildup on that edge.

Chapter 8
Organic Versus Nonorganic Vegetable Gardening

You've already learned the basics for growing healthy organic vegetables. You know when and where to plant your vegetables, how to space out your plants, and what to feed them. But it's worth discussing organic growing methods—and nonorganic alternatives—in more detail. Organic gardening uses practices that help to restore and maintain harmony with nature, which include feeding the soil. Nonorganic or conventional practices use chemicals and pesticides to help plants grow. In this chapter, we will discuss the differences between growing your vegetables organically versus nonorganically.

What Is Organic Gardening?

Gardening without using synthetic fertilizers and pesticides can be considered organic gardening. In organic gardening, the motto "feed the soil, feed the plant" is the basis for growing your vegetables. This means bringing in a minimal amount of off-site additions into your garden. Making your own compost and growing cover crops when your garden is idle are two easy ways to accomplish this.

✳ *Smoothie Garden Solution*

Overall, there are not many disadvantages to organic growing, but it can take a lot of planning and can be labor intensive. Sustaining good soil fertility takes work and commitment. It can take time to identify the source of infestations and find natural ways to deal with them, which obviously takes longer than simply spraying a chemical to kill them.

The restoration, preservation, and enrichment of the soil are the cornerstones of organic gardening. All plants need four basic requirements to grow: warmth, moisture, food, and light. Your garden soil provides the first three and the sun provides the fourth! The soil is a living system that needs care and attention to remain in a healthy enough state to provide plants with the nutrients they need to grow and produce vegetables.

Maintaining a healthy, fertile garden soil is extremely important to having a successful vegetable garden. Building good soil starts with knowing what soil type you have and how fertile it is. You then need to regularly use certain methods, such as adding amendments every season, rotating your crops, and growing cover crops to enhance your existing soil. If your existing soil is poor, it can take several years to get your garden beds to a state of high fertility and good structure, but do not let that discourage you. Some very successful vegetable gardens started out with sandy or rocky soil!

✳ *Smoothie Garden Solution*

Earthworms will gradually make an acidic soil less acid and an alkaline soil less alkaline by passing the soil through their bodies. They will eventually bring soil that is out of balance back to the neutral pH range. Most vegetables grow best in a pH range of 6.0 to 6.9.

In nonorganic or conventional methods, synthetic chemicals and pesticides are used to enhance the growth of the plant and to promote fruit or pod production. Nonorganic growing methods emphasize feeding the plant, not the soil. Using these artificial forms will make your vegetables grow, but they also deplete and will not enhance the soil fertility or soil structure. Most conventional growers have dead soil; there are no replenished nutrients in the soil for the plants to draw from. Relying on something outside your soil to grow vegetable plants creates a vicious circle. You have to purchase more and more chemicals and pesticides in order for the crops to grow each season.

The Organic Principles

The International Federation of Organic Agricultural Movements has laid out a list of principles of organic farming. It emphasizes growing high quality food, considering the social and ecological impact of organic food production, promoting natural biological cycles within the farming systems, optimizing the long-term soil fertility, minimizing pollution, and using water resources responsibly.

Most gardeners grow vegetables so they can eat them. Everyone wants to get the best possible harvest from their seeds or transplants. The best way to do this is to try to copy what nature does as closely as you can. The forest is a perfect example of how plants remain healthy and vibrant without any outside additions. In the forest, the seasons and the natural relationships between plants and animals create a healthy soil. With a vegetable garden, you have to work a bit more in order to get the same results. You can accomplish this by feeding the soil compost, animal manures, leaves, and other organic matter.

When growing in your backyard, it is important to consider other living creatures in the area. For example, encouraging birds, wasps, and bees will help deter pests. You can assist the natural cycle of life by including plants that encourage and attract certain insects in your garden.

You are helping the environment and minimizing pollution by growing your own vegetables. For every vegetable you grow and eat yourself, you are saving fuel that would be used to bring that item to you. By composting your kitchen scraps or garden waste, you support the environment by not adding to landfills. Most waste is either burned or buried, and both methods affect our environment.

✳ *Smoothie Garden Solution*

Aquatic animals such as toads, box turtles, and frogs love to eat insects, so encourage their presence in your garden. For a shelter, place a clay flowerpot upside down in your garden and chip the side to make a little space for them to enter. Make a pond or fill a shallow container with water to give them a source of water.

Another principle in organic gardening is creating a harmonious balance between vegetable production and animal husbandry. Chickens and larger animals such as cows, pigs, and sheep are a fabulous complement to vegetable gardening. And you don't have to live in a rural area to take advantage of this balance. Chickens are allowed in backyards in some cities, so check your local regulations.

Animal manures are a great amendment to any garden soil. Chicken manure is especially high in nitrogen, which your vegetable plants need to grow healthy green leaves. Just make sure you let the manure age for at least six months before adding it to your garden bed or it will burn your vegetable plants. If you do have animals either as pets or for slaughter, it is important to treat them humanely. They deserve to have proper food and shelter.

Encouraging certain wildlife to enter your garden site is probably not the wisest choice. One deer or elk can devour a whole garden in a single night. Ensure that these animals stay wild by erecting a proper fence to protect your garden and still allow them access to the grass and weeds nearby.

✳ *Smoothie Garden Solution*

There are 115 species of snakes in North America, and only four are poisonous. Most of the ones you find in your garden will only bite if you pick them up or step on them, and their bites are largely harmless. The common garter snake, eastern ribbon snake, western terrestrial snake, green snake, and brown snake will eat slugs, snails, and insects.

Maintaining and promoting a healthy use of water is another one of the organic principles. Using proper methods for watering your vegetables will produce healthier plants without depleting our water resources. Gardeners often give their plants more water than is necessary, so take the time to check the soil to see if it really needs water. Use drip irrigation or soaker hoses rather than sprinklers to save on the amount of water that is wasted through evaporation.

The Benefits of Eating Organic

There are many reasons to choose to grow and eat organically grown vegetables. Organic food is healthier than food grown with pesticides and chemicals. It has higher levels of vitamin C and other minerals such as calcium, iron, chromium, and magnesium. Organic vegetables are normally harvested when ripe and are therefore tastier, more flavorful, and more nutritious.

Organic foods that are processed do not contain any food additives or artificial hormones, which contribute to health problems such as migraines, heart disease, and obesity. Children are much more susceptible to chemicals and pesticides added to vegetables and other products. Choosing to grow and eat organically grown vegetables is one way to keep your family healthier.

In conventional or nonorganic growing, vegetables are routinely sprayed with more than 400 chemical pesticides. They harm the person who eats the food and the person who grows it. They do nothing to replenish the soil to help it stay healthy and remain fertile. Genetically modified organism (GMO) crops are not allowed under organic standards but are commonly used in nonorganic or conventional growing methods. These seeds have not been tested on humans, so the long-term effects of eating them are still unknown.

✳ Smoothie Garden Solution

Foods that meet the U.S. Department of Agriculture's requirements for organic production will have a USDA seal. To obtain the seal, foods must be 95 percent organic. Foods using only organic products and methods may also state "100% organic" on the packaging. A lower level of organic certification is available for foods that are 70 to 95 percent organic. These foods can be labeled as "made with organic ingredients."

Choosing to grow your own vegetables and committing to growing them using organic principles and methods will give you the assurance of knowing what you are eating. It is also becoming more popular to purchase vegetables, fruits, and other products that are grown and made in your local community or area. Because of this new trend, there are more small growers—even some backyard gardeners are growing extra vegetables to sell at farmers' markets or gate sales. If growing veggies is something you love to do, you might be able to earn a living doing it. If you have the desire and time to grow vegetables, the extra money is a huge bonus—as is the satisfaction of selling fresh produce that others will enjoy.

✳ Smoothie Garden Solution

Maximize a small space by interplanting a variety of vegetables within a certain area. Grow combinations of fast-growing varieties with vegetables that take longer to mature. Grow lettuce with corn, peas, or tomatoes. Grow beans with carrots, corn, or cucumbers. Grow radishes with onions, peas, or carrots.

The Transition

If you are a gardener who has not been growing organically and has decided to make some changes, there are a few easy ways to make the transition. A vegetable garden can take a fair amount of care and attention. If you are transitioning from nonorganic to organic growing, be patient with yourself and your garden. Change can be difficult on all living things—remember, your soil and plants are living organisms. Commit to using the organic method, and when the process seems difficult, remember that you are enhancing the health of your family and the planet. You will soon see positive results with happier vegetable, fewer pests, and more beneficial insects and birds to enjoy.

Commit to Organic Gardening

First, make the commitment to growing using organic methods. If you are hesitant to change, start with a small area and transition more space each year. If you have decided to go organic right now, the first thing you must do is throw out any pesticides or chemicals you may have in your garden shed or garage. Take them to a place where they can be disposed of responsibly. Check with your local waste management site for the best way to destroy them.

Start with Soil Investigation

Get a soil test to check the current nutrient amount and fertility of your soil. Research the organic fertilizers that are available at your local garden center. Look for blood meal, alfalfa meal, bone meal, kelp, rock phosphate, and greensand. These are all excellent products to add to your soil in the spring a few weeks before you start planting.

Start a Compost Pile

Compost is one of the foundations of organic gardening. Use your kitchen waste, garden waste, leaves, and grass clippings. Rather than throwing them into the garbage, use them to make an excellent amendment for your garden soil.

❋ *Smoothie Garden Solution*

Steep slopes where rainfall can wash away soil are not the best place to plant your vegetable garden. A slight slope will work if you plant your rows across the slope. On level ground, run your rows north to south to maximize exposure to the sun.

Collect Organic Matter

No matter how fertile your soil is, you will always need to add in organic matter on a regular basis as the plants use up the nutrients in the existing soil. Your garden soil will always need to be replenished. Contact local farms that may have animal manure for you to use. Some may charge for it, others may give it away, and still others will give it away if you come and clean out the pens! Try to get as much as you can.

Plan Your Crop Rotation

Planting your vegetables in a new area each year is an important aspect of organic gardening. This helps prevent pests and disease and keeps your soil healthier.

Plant Cover Crops

Cover crops are an inexpensive way to add organic matter to your garden soil. These are green plants that are usually planted in the fall and turned under in early spring. The green tops and plant roots add the organic matter to the soil. There are a variety of crops you can grow depending on what type of soil you have and what you want the crop to ultimately do for the soil. They can be used to add nitrogen to the soil, prevent weeds from growing, or just to add in lots of organic matter, which will decompose into a rich humus material. Check with your local garden center or any seed catalog for the varieties that are available for your area.

✳ Smoothie Garden Solution

Even in a small garden, leave space between your garden rows so you can walk and work between them. In large vegetable gardens, make paths and leave enough space at the end of rows so you can easily turn a cultivator and wheelbarrows.

Use Mulches

Mulches are used in organic growing to help protect the garden soil from getting too wet, becoming too dry, and eroding. Straw, hay, shredded leaves, and grass clippings are all common mulch materials. These items are all organic matter, which will decompose over time and add to the fertility of your garden soil. If your cover crop gets too high (more than six inches), cut or mow it before tilling it under and use the green matter as mulch in another area of your garden.

Chapter 9
Harvesting Your Bounty

Enjoying fresh, tasty veggies from your own garden is the highlight of having a garden. You'll be amazed at how much better your smoothies taste when they're made from vegetables that you've grown and harvested. Vegetables mature at different times; some are best picked early, some late, and still others need to be harvested regularly or the plant will stop producing. All this variation can make it difficult to know when to start harvesting. In this chapter you will learn how to recognize when your plants are ready to be picked, which ones will keep producing for you, which storage methods will keep everything fresh, and which plants are best for freezing and canning for winter use.

Tips for an Easy Harvest

We are usually impatient to have our fruit, pods, and seeds ripe enough to eat. Eating fresh veggies is the reason for having a garden. The taste and crunchiness of freshly picked veggies is a real treat that you are not aware of until you actually do it.

Observation is the best way to learn when to harvest your veggies. If you are really organized, you can make a note on the calendar based on the maturity date of the variety you planted. For most gardeners this is too much work, so "pick and taste" is probably the best test to see if your veggies are ready to be eaten. If you harvest too early they may lack sweetness, size, and flavor. If you wait too long, many vegetables lose their flavor, become starchy-tasting, and are tough. For instance, peas and corn become starchy-tasting when older. Beans can become stringy and zucchini seems to become monster-size overnight if not picked regularly.

Along with zucchini squash, other plants such as peas and beans need to be harvested regularly so the plant will keep producing more. If the pods or fruit are not harvested in a timely way, the vegetable plants will take that as a signal to stop producing and will start producing flowers and seeds rather than new fruits or pods.

✳ *Smoothie Garden Solution*

Thinning plants provides more room to grow. When direct-seeding it is difficult to know how many seedlings will germinate; however, it is important to pull out some of the seedlings to give the rest a better chance to grow. Check the seed packet for suggested spacing of plants.

Use sharp tools to harvest your veggies. Some fruit can be easily pulled or broken off, which can damage the plants and they will not produce anything more for you.

It is generally a good idea to harvest early in the morning when there is still dew on the plants, especially leafy vegetables like lettuce or other greens. That way they stay fresher and keep longer. For root crops, it is great to have a bucket of water handy to quickly wash off the dirt. Otherwise you are tracking it inside the house. Use the muddy water to water your containers or other plants.

Harvesting can be fun and a great way to get your family together. Tasting as you pick is totally okay! Make it an event. If you have lots of veggies, get your neighbors involved and share the pickings or make a meal together with some of the harvested veggies. Canning is another great way to get a group of friends together to have fun now and enjoy later.

Knowing When to Pick Your Veggies

Different vegetables are harvested at different times and in many different ways. Certain vegetables need to be harvested on a regular basis to keep the plant producing more. Some you harvest at the peak of ripeness and the plant only produces one item; others will keep producing a crop over several weeks, and still others will produce a second crop but in smaller sizes.

Salad Veggies

Salad vegetables such as arugula, romaine, radicchio, spinach, Swiss chard, Oriental greens, and salad greens can be harvested by cutting individual baby leaves or cutting the mature plants. For baby greens to be used in salads, cut when the leaves are two to three inches high. Do not disturb the roots. That way another set of greens will grow. You can usually get two cuttings before the plant will stop producing or start tasting bitter. For a mature plant, check the seed packet to see how long the variety is supposed to take to mature; if left too long, lettuce can have a bitter taste. A mature plant can be cut off at the base of the plant or individual leaves can be cut as well (most common in Swiss chard). Cut the outer leaves, leaving the center to produce more leaves; if the roots are not disturbed, the plant will grow again. A sign that the plant is finished producing is when the center stalk starts to grow taller and the flowers start to form. You can pinch off the flower and the leaves can still be eaten; however, they can start to become bitter once the flower starts growing.

❋ *Smoothie Garden Solution*

To keep lettuce longer, moisten a clean kitchen towel and wrap it around the lettuce. Place this into a plastic bag and put it in the refrigerator. Do not seal the bag as it will keep better with air circulation. The lettuce will keep for up to two weeks stored this way.

Brassicas

Brassicas, sometimes also known as the cabbage family, include your cabbages, broccoli, and cauliflower. This family of vegetable plants usually produces one good-size head. Some will keep producing smaller heads once the main one has been harvested. These vegetables can be harvested once the head reaches approximately four to eight inches in diameter, with the variety, your soil fertility, and garden conditions often determining the size of the head.

For broccoli you want to harvest the head when it is a bright green color and still firm. Once it starts to open, it is beginning to flower and will be less flavorful. Once you cut the center head, broccoli will produce side shoots off the main stem, and if cut regularly, can produce more shoots for several weeks. These will be considerably smaller in size and will go to flower quickly if not cut. Cauliflower will produce only one head. Make sure the head is filled out and firm before harvesting it. It is getting old when the florets start to open. The opening means the plant is starting to flower.

Peas and Beans

Peas and beans are two of the crops that are best picked on the early side as they are usually sweeter and tender when small. Common pea varieties grown are shelling peas (for the seed inside the pod), flat snow peas used fresh or for cooking, and the snap variety, which is grown for the crunchy pod. You want the pea pods to be full and for the pod to be easily opened if it is a shelling pea or sweet and crunchy if it is an edible pod variety. Once they get older the pods become wrinkly and the pea seeds begin to taste bitter and starchy. Once your peas are ready for harvesting, pick them every few days or the plant will stop producing more. Leave some pods on the plant to fill out completely; then shell the peas, dry, and save them for planting next season.

Fresh cucumbers taste so much better than ones bought in the store and they are easy to grow. They're also an essential component of many green smoothies. Cucumbers can be trellised, which is great when growing in small spaces. There are slicing varieties, which are harvested when they are six to twelve inches long; check the packet for the size at maturity. Depending on the variety, some cucumbers are eaten with the skin on like the English cucumber, whereas others are peeled and the inner white flesh is sliced. You want to pick cucumbers regularly so that the plant keeps producing more.

For winter squash it is best to leave the fruit on the vine as long as you can; often a frost will make the squash even sweeter-tasting. A quick test to see if they are ready to be harvested is pricking the skin with your fingernail. If it leaves an indentation, it is not ready; if there is no mark on the skin, the fruit can be harvested.

Root Vegetables

Root veggies are the plants that can be left in the ground such as carrots and beets. The advantage to growing root crops is that you can harvest as you need them rather than having to eat them up as soon as they mature. Carrots, beets, rutabaga, and potatoes can be harvested as small as you want them to be. Pulling baby carrots or beets helps to make room in the row for the rest of the plants to grow larger. Baby veggies are often sweeter tasting; however, the flavor of root crops usually does not change that much as they mature; they will just grow bigger. Most root crops can be left in the ground over winter so long as the soil does not get too wet and the plants are well mulched so they do not freeze.

Heat-Loving Vegetables

Heat-loving veggies such as tomatoes, cucumbers, and corn all have specific indicators that tell if the vegetable is ready for picking or not. Peppers can be harvested at pretty much any size, usually when they are three inches or so in diameter. They also start out as green and are very often harvested at this stage; however, if they are left on the plant, they will turn red, orange, or yellow depending on the variety. For them to change color, you have to be patient. It can take several weeks once the green pepper is at its full size before it will have fully changed color.

✳ *Smoothie Garden Solution*

The secret to a healthy pepper with good color and flavor is adequate water and fertilizer! The pepper plant does not need a lot of nitrogen—this will promote leaf growth but not fruits. Keep the plants mulched with grass clippings to keep the soil moist and weed-free.

All heat-loving vegetables such as tomatoes, peppers, eggplant, and cucumbers will keep producing over several weeks if you continue to harvest the fruit. The exception to this is corn. Each stalk will produce one or two cobs and that is all. Before you harvest corn you want the cob to be filled out and firm to the touch. Gently pull away some of the husk and see if the kernels are a bright yellow (some varieties are white or a mix of yellow and white). If they look fully formed and are a good color gently prick the kernels with your fingernail. If a milky liquid shoots out they are ready to be harvested.

Storage Tips

You cannot buy vegetables with the kind of flavor and nutrition that you get from growing and harvesting your own. Since most people garden only seasonally, it is really great to be able to have some of our vegetables in the off-season. If you have enough veggies for your immediate smoothie needs, and if you want to feed your family with your fresh veggies all year long, it is important to start at the planning stage. Make sure you estimate how much you will eat fresh and how much you would like to store, freeze, or can, and then plant accordingly. The natural course is for the vegetables eventually to rot, so it is important to store them properly to slow down the aging process. The next step is learning how and where to store and how to preserve these veggies.

Some vegetables like salad greens have a very short life and need to be refrigerated until you're ready to use them in a smoothie. They will last for only a week at the most, whereas other vegetables like winter squash, potatoes, and onions, if cured properly, will store for several months.

The following are vegetables to store in the refrigerator unwashed and to use as soon as possible:

- Asparagus

- Broccoli

- Greens—collards, spinach, salad greens, lettuce, kale, Swiss chard

- Peas

Here are vegetables to store in a cool and damp area:

- Beets

- Brussels sprouts

- Carrots

- Peppers

Store these vegetables in a cool and dry area:

- Garlic

- Onions

You will need to have a proper storage space for the types of vegetables you want to store. If you are storing for resale, proper coolers that regulate temperature and humidity will be needed. However, for the home gardener this equipment is very costly and not necessary. If you are lucky enough to have an existing root cellar, it is a great place to store produce as it is usually cool, dry, and dark. A cool, dry area in your basement or a pantry will work just as well.

Which Veggies Can I Freeze?

Freezing your vegetables to use during the winter months is a great way to eat healthy all year long and to save money. If there is a certain veggie you love, plan in advance to make sure you plant a sufficient amount so you can freeze some to enjoy later. You may get a bumper crop of a certain vegetable, and freezing or canning is a great way to use the produce so it does not go to waste. Freezing will preserve the nutrients and flavor of the vegetables.

When you are planning to freeze your produce, pick it and freeze it the same day. That way you will be getting the full nutrients when you eat the food later. It is best to pick the veggies early in the morning when the temperature is lower. Choose the freshest and most tender veggies, and then keep them cool until they can be put into the freezer. If left at room temperature for more than two hours, the vegetables start to lose their nutrients so you want to work fast to preserve them.

FREEZING AND BLANCHING	
VEGETABLES THAT WILL FREEZE WELL	AMOUNT OF TIME FOR BLANCHING
Asparagus	2 minutes
Beet, collard, spinach, Swiss chard greens	2 minutes
Broccoli	3 minutes
Carrots	5 minutes for whole; 3 minutes for sliced or diced
Corn	4 minutes for whole cob; 1 minute for kernels
Peas	1 minute

Blanching, also known as scalding, is done to destroy enzymes in your vegetables. Enzymes will affect the color and flavor of your vegetables if they are kept frozen for any length of time. If you are planning to eat your frozen veggies such as string beans, peas, or small carrots within a month, you do not necessarily have to blanch these items. However, if you will be eating them over the winter, take the time to scald your vegetables as they will look and taste better when you get around to eating them.

To blanch your harvested vegetables, fill a pot with water and bring it to a fast boil. You can add a few teaspoons of lemon juice or salt to your boiling water to help with discoloration. Use a wire rack to hold the vegetables and lower them into the boiling water. Start timing immediately and closely watch the time, as just one minute over will give you mushy vegetables. Most vegetables will take one to four minutes (check the list just given for timing). You then need to plunge the vegetables into ice-cold water for the same amount of time as you blanched them to stop the cooking process. Continue the process with each batch of vegetables, making sure the water is at a fast boil and adding more ice to the water for cooling. Drain the vegetables and then place them on a tray or cookie sheet and put them in the freezer for an hour or so. After that time you can portion them into bags or containers and return them to the freezer. This method prevents any water crystals from forming in your bags or containers.

✳ *Smoothie Garden Solution*

Your vegetables will not improve in quality when frozen, so if you are freezing produce that has been sitting around for a few days, or was on the old side when it was harvested, the quality will not magically change. Choose the freshest vegetables to freeze!

Labeling is an essential part of freezing your vegetables unless you like the mystery of what is in the package! You can use whatever labeling system works for you. Use a felt pen and write on the bag or container, purchase peel-and-stick labels, or get really creative and color code each type of vegetable with a colored label. Label the top of the container if you have a chest freezer and the front if you have an upright freezer.

Chapter 10
Plan for Next Season

Planning is one of the essential elements of a successful vegetable garden. Knowing what worked and did not work will help you to plan and avoid the same problems. Take time during the year to document what happened. At the end of the season, you can evaluate what worked well and what you would like to do differently. Apply the questions in this chapter to your own vegetable garden and your experiences.

Did You Choose a Good Garden Site?

Go over the questions you answered in Chapter 1 to start your garden. Do you still agree with your reasons for starting a garden or have they changed? What did you like about the site you picked? What would you change about it? If the site did not work well, evaluate different sites or different gardening methods. If you chose to grow in your backyard but found you preferred to grow in containers, maybe you can plan to use more containers next year. Were you satisfied with all of your vegetables? Would you like to grow different vegetables? More vegetables? Fewer vegetables?

✳ *Smoothie Garden Solution*

There is always something new to learn about your garden site and growing vegetables. Take a course at your local community center, go on gardening tours, take a seminar, or join a gardening club. These are all fabulous ways to learn more and connect with fellow gardeners.

If you reinvented an old site or grew in an existing garden what worked and what did not? What would you need to do to make it even better next year? Gardening is always a work in progress. Plants grow and die back, some do better than others in your soil conditions, the weather and sunlight affect how plants grow, and unexpected problems always crop up. By taking the time to revisit your gardening season, you can write down ideas and plans for next season. We all think we will remember, but more often than not the small details are what can make your gardening life easier. Those little things are what you need to write down!

Did Your Plants Get Enough Sunlight and Rainfall?

Most vegetable plants need an average of six hours of sunlight a day and one inch of water every week to grow their best.

Did your site get the amount of sunlight you thought it would? If not, can you move your garden to another area? What other changes can you make? The sun shifts over the season, so what was in full sun in the spring may not have been in the summer and fall months. Do you need to plan your vegetable plantings to take advantage of this? If you know part of your garden is going to be in shade in the hot summer months, perhaps your lettuces will do better in a given spot than your tomatoes. Take time to re-examine your garden rotation.

✳ *Smoothie Garden Solution*

Gardening can be a very creative pursuit. Designing and planning your vegetable garden layout each season can be a way to express your creativity. Use your creative or artistic abilities to create structures, sculptures, or use garden ornaments to make your garden special for you and your family.

Water, like sunlight, is essential for growing vegetables. Did you take into account the amount of rainfall you did or did not get? When you watered was it an easy or a difficult process? Do you need to make changes on how you watered your veggies? How you water certain vegetable plants can affect how they grow and what pests or diseases they may attract. Now is the time to make a list of any new hoses, water wands, or nozzles you have or may want to purchase for next season. The best sales are often in the fall, when you do not need to water!

Was the Garden Too Large or Too Small?

Novice gardeners in particular find it challenging to assess the resources they need to plant, grow, maintain, and harvest a vegetable garden. How did you do? If you struggled to keep the area you had in reasonable shape, do not feel bad about scaling back a bit. If you started out small and feel you can easily go larger, then take the time to see how best to expand your garden site.

Weeds are often easy to control in a new garden site. When an area is newly tilled, weed seeds are often killed off. In other cases, the soil may not be as fertile, so the weeds do not grow as well. But beware. In the second or third season, weeds often seem to get out of control. Take that into consideration if you want to expand your garden. Once you start adding compost and amendments to your garden soil, both your veggies and your weeds will grow faster and bigger. If you can't decide whether to expand, try growing in the same-size area for a second season and then make your decision.

✳ *Smoothie Garden Solution*

You can make money vegetable gardening! Some gardeners garden as a hobby, but there are others who earn a living by growing and selling vegetables. If this is something you want to pursue, check out your local farmers' markets or roadside stands to see what others are doing and talk to them to see how they got started.

The fall is a great time to change the size of your vegetable garden. If you need to till a larger area, do it in the fall, adding in as much compost and aged animal manure as you can get your hands on. Plant a cover crop if you have time or add in some mulch to keep the nutrients from leaching out. In the spring, you will have a fertile garden bed ready to be planted! On the other hand, if you find you have taken on more than you could handle, the fall is a perfect time to plant some grass seed or perennial flowers and shrubs into the vegetable garden beds you won't use again next year.

Did You Have Too Many or Too Few Vegetables?

Did you and your family eat what you grew? Did you plant too much or too little of any vegetables? Were you surprised about what grew really well or did poorly? Did the family like something you tried as an experiment? Jot down notes so you remember what you want to plant next season.

Be careful not to mistake a bumper crop for overplanting. The perfect soil conditions and the perfect amount of water, sunlight, and heat can give you an overabundance of a certain vegetable. If you planted four cucumber plants and had too many for your use, think about scaling down to three plants. If you still have too many cucumbers the second season, perhaps you have the perfect garden for cucumbers! You can then scale back a bit more. However, remember that each year may bring different challenges, so plant at least two of everything to ensure you will have some veggies to eat.

✳ *Smoothie Garden Solution*

Growing healthy, safe food is a priority for some gardeners. Because there are more food scares in the world and more product recalls, it is more important than ever to know where your food is grown. If you can grow your own vegetables and fruits, you will create a healthier life for yourself and your family.

Is there anything you can do to improve the growing conditions of the veggies that did not do so well? Not every vegetable will grow well in every site. Certain vegetables need more warmth, sunlight, or protection from the elements than others. Would certain plants do better in a container on your front patio than in the backyard? Do you need a greenhouse or cold frame to give your plants that extra warmth they need? If a vegetable plant consistently does not do well in your garden, try growing it in another way or acknowledge your site is just not what that plant needs. It does not mean anything about you as a gardener!

Did You Have Pest Problems?

It never fails. You finally feel you have vanquished the pests in your garden and something new shows up! No garden is pest-free—nor do you necessarily want it to be. There are beneficial and harmful pests and they both need to coexist for a healthy vegetable garden.

What is important is to document your problem pests, what you did to prevent or get rid of them, and your results. This is valuable information to have for the seasons to come, although not every season will have the same problems. If something worked one season it will probably work again. If, however, something did not work, you do not want to waste your time doing the same thing again next season!

❋ *Smoothie Garden Solution*

Gardening can be a very pleasurable experience. Having a vegetable or flower garden in your backyard, patio, or balcony can add beauty to your home. Plants can attract wildlife, birds, butterflies, and other insects that are beautiful to watch and enjoy. Take the time to really experience your garden.

Tilling your garden beds is one way to expose any insects and larvae to the elements, which will make it harder for them to survive. Planting a cover crop or using mulch will keep your soil healthy. Keeping your plants healthier makes it easier for them to fight off any harmful pests. Once the garden is winding down in the fall, put up new fences or fix the ones that were not working to keep out any unwanted animals.

Were Certain Diseases a Problem?

If your vegetable plants have a certain disease one year, they will most likely get it again. Diseases that affect plants are often soil-borne diseases that are very difficult to get rid of. But there are ways to prevent or at least minimize the effect they have on your vegetable plants. If you have diseased vegetable plants, try to identify the problem and research its cause. The more information you can get on the disease, the better equipped you will be to prevent it next season.

Some gardeners feel intimidated and disheartened if they have problems in their vegetable garden. Rather than letting the problem ruin your gardening experience, see it as a learning experience or an adventure. If your garden site is susceptible to a certain disease, try growing varieties that are resistant to that particular problem, or do not grow that vegetable at all. Gardening will be more fun if you are not fighting the same issue every year!

✳ *Smoothie Garden Solution*

Gardens can offer a spiritual connection for some people. Your vegetable garden can be a tranquil retreat where you can escape from the outside world. Take a stroll around your garden to lift your spirits and release the stress or anxiety you may be holding onto. Sit and take in the peace and beauty all around you!

Keeping your garden clean is one of the best ways to prevent disease. In the fall, make sure you clean up any debris in and around your garden beds. Either plant a cover crop or mulch the area to prevent any soil erosion and leaching of the nutrients in the soil. If you have veggies growing all winter long, make sure you take care of them so you won't invite problems for next season.

Did You Have the Tools You Needed?

As a new gardener, good quality tools can be expensive. Buying a good tool every season may be the most economical way to get everything you want. Now that you have a growing season under your belt, you can make your list of what you need and a separate wish list. Proper tools for the job and the proper fit for the gardener can make vegetable gardening more fun and easier on the body.

The fall is a great time to make your list and catch some sales. It is also very important to take care of the tools you already have. Keeping tools clean all season long is a habit every gardener should have. Tools also need to be stored properly for the winter. If you do not have a garage or garden shed, find another protected area to store them—under a patio, under your front steps, attached to a wall that has an overhanging eave, or even under a large tree covered with a tarp to keep them somewhat protected from the weather.

✳ Smoothie Garden Solution

Use your garden to expand your social circle. Gardening is a great way to meet your neighbors and get involved in your community. Give extra vegetables to the local food bank or soup kitchen or organize a neighborhood party. Have everyone bring a dish of food made from something they grew in their backyard!

What Do You Want to Try Next Season?

Imagine your perfect vegetable garden. What do you see in your perfect garden next season? What steps do you need to take to make it that way? Review what worked or did not work and choose to make changes that will make it more of what you want. Small and inexpensive changes can make a huge difference to how your garden looks and how well the vegetables grow. It is fun to experiment with planting vegetables that may not be common to your area or trying a new variety.

Trying something new can renew your interest if the garden is becoming a bit stale or your interest is waning. If you have a wild area and prefer a manicured garden, it may take some money and effort to make it happen, but it can be done. If you have recently moved into a new home and the garden is not quite to your taste, now is the time to make plans to change things. It may take several seasons, but it all starts with a dream and then a plan of action.

✳ Smoothie Garden Solution

Most of us have childhood memories about food or gardening. Gardening is a fun way for the family to spend time together and for children to learn how to grow vegetables. Gardens are where memories are made.

Adjust the garden to changes in your life. If you have welcomed a new child, taken on a more demanding job, or retired, reassess how much time, energy, and money you'll be able to put into your garden. Be realistic, and you'll have a more enjoyable gardening experience.

Did You Have Fun?

There are many reasons for having a vegetable garden. Gardening can give you food, exercise, and pleasure. It can help you meet your neighbors, make money, be creative, relax, and establish family time. These are all wonderful reasons, but you also need to have fun and enjoy the tasks involved in growing a successful vegetable garden. Gardening can be hard work and there is a lot to learn, especially as a beginner. The best advice is to start small. Start with a tiny patch that you can easily handle and cannot wait to get back to every spring.

Part II

Growing Green Smoothie Vegetables and Herbs

Chapter 11
Leaf Vegetables

Greens are plants that produce leaves quickly and are often harvested before the plant reaches maturity. Lettuces and salad green mixes are some of the easiest vegetables to grow in a small-space garden. They grow in various shades of greens and reds and have different flavors, which they can lend to your smoothie repertoire. You want your smoothie stuff to grow rapidly for best flavor, so they require a rich soil high in nitrogen and need to be well watered. In this chapter you will get information and easy growing tips for lettuce, radicchio, romaine, spinach, and watercress.

For a positive effect, plant your leaf vegetables with beets, cabbage, peas, clover, and radishes. There are no plants that have a negative effect on these lettuce plants.

✳ *Smoothie Garden Solution*

Overseeding is probably one of the biggest problems in growing leaf vegetables. If seeds are broadcasted (sowed over a wide area by hand), they will need to be thinned. One of the best ways to do this is to treat your garden bed as a transplant bed. As plants come up, gently move the seedlings to other areas of your garden.

Lettuce

Lettuce is one of the most common vegetables for the home gardener, and it's very easy to grow. There are several types and varieties of lettuce you can choose to grow, including leaf lettuce, Bibb lettuce, romaine lettuce, and iceberg lettuce. With some leaf varieties, you can cut the outer leaves to eat, leaving the center to produce more new growth. You can also let the lettuce plant reach maturity and then cut the whole head at the base of the plant. Plan to plant several different varieties of lettuce in your garden so you can enjoy tasty and colorful salads.

Lettuce

Lettuce is a cool-season vegetable and can be planted as soon as you can get into your garden. It grows great in containers on a patio or balcony as well. All types of lettuce have the same growing requirements. You want your lettuce to grow rapidly for best flavor, so a nitrogen-rich soil is best. Add nitrogen-rich fertilizer such as blood meal, alfalfa meal, or aged chicken manure during the soil preparation. Lettuce plants have quite shallow roots, so you only need to add a few inches of compost or aged manure to the garden bed. You want the soil to be moist but well drained. Lettuce does not like soggy or saturated soil.

Lettuce can be planted almost anywhere in your garden. It is a fast-growing vegetable, so you get quick results. To have lettuce all season long, start a few plants indoors in early spring. When you transplant those out to the garden, plant more seeds. Do this every few weeks. A great way to get the most out of your garden space is to plant some lettuce seeds or transplants under slower-growing vegetables such as cabbage, cauliflower, and broccoli. These larger plants will give the lettuce plants the shade they need during the summer months.

QUICK TIPS FOR GROWING LETTUCE

EDIBLE PARTS	Leaves and stems.
LOCATION	Shady area with a cool temperature. Lettuce grows well in raised beds and containers.
BEST SOIL	Loose, rich, well drained; pH 6.0–6.8.
WHEN TO PLANT	For transplants sow indoors early March to mid-July; direct-seed as soon as you can work your soil and plant more every few weeks.
HOW TO PLANT	Can be transplanted or sown directly to the garden. Sow seeds ¼-inch deep, spacing them 8 to 10 inches apart in rows 12 to 24 inches apart.
HOW MUCH TO PLANT	10 to 15 plants per person each season.
WEEDING	Keep the area around the plant well weeded.
WATERING	Drip irrigation or overhead sprinkling will work well. Plants need 1 to 2 inches each week and may require more if the weather is hot. Sprinkling the leaves in the early morning will help to keep the plant cooler during the hot part of the day.
CARE	Provide some shade in the heat of the summer. A floating row cover works well.
FERTILIZING	Add compost tea or fish fertilizer around the base of the plant every 2 to 3 weeks after planting.
PESTS AND DISEASES	Use crop rotation as prevention. Some common pests and diseases include slugs, aphids, cabbage loopers, flea beetles, downy mildew, and fusarium wilt.
WHEN TO HARVEST	Lettuce plants reach maturity at between 50 to 75 days. Harvest leaf and romaine lettuce when the plant is large enough to use. Harvest Bibb lettuce when a loose head is formed and iceberg lettuce when the head is firm.
HOW TO HARVEST	Cut or pull off leaves of leaf lettuce. For head lettuce varieties, use a sharp knife to cut off the heads at the base of the plant.

QUICK TIPS FOR GROWING LETTUCE	
STORAGE	Wash leaves, dry them in a salad spinner, and place them in a sealed plastic bag or container. They will store well for up to 1 week in the refrigerator.

Radicchio

Radicchio is a great smoothie ingredient. Its brilliant red and white leaves give the smoothie a nice color, and radicchio has a bite that is absent in other lettuces.

QUICK TIPS FOR GROWING RADICCHIO	
FAMILY NAME	Asteraceae (aster, daisy, or sunflower family).
EDIBLE PARTS	Leaves.
LOCATION	Does well in full sun or light shade.
BEST SOIL	Fertile, rich soil; enclosed beds are fine.
WHEN TO PLANT	Either spring or fall; radicchio likes cold weather, so plant in the spring up to four weeks before your expected last frost.
HOW TO PLANT	Sow the seeds ¼-inch under the soil. You can thin as they start to grow. If you're transplanting from pots or seedbeds, plant 12 to 14 inches apart.
HOW MUCH TO PLANT	4 to 5 plants per person.
WEEDING	Keep the area around the plants weed-free.
WATERING	Frequent light watering.
FERTILIZING	A low-grade nitrogen blend is okay; compost tea around the site after planting.

QUICK TIPS FOR GROWING RADICCHIO	
PESTS AND DISEASES	Caterpillars and slugs prey on radicchio leaves; use saucers of beer to keep them at bay. Aphids attack the larger veins in the plant leaves; use natural pyrethrin-based sprays against them.
WHEN TO HARVEST	Pick the leaves after the first few light frosts.
HOW TO HARVEST	You can cut the leaves you're going to use in your smoothie; radicchio is a perennial, so after your first planting you'll be able to enjoy their leaves for years to come.
STORAGE	Store in a plastic bag with a damp paper towel to keep it moist. But the best thing is to pick only enough leaves to toss into your smoothie immediately.

Romaine

Romaine, the base green of Caesar salad, is also a wonderful component of smoothies. Its bright green leaves are sweet to the taste and will fill out any smoothie you make.

QUICK TIPS FOR GROWING ROMAINE	
FAMILY NAME	Asteraceae (aster, daisy, or sunflower family).
EDIBLE PARTS	Leaves.
LOCATION	Full sun in the early summer; light shade mid-summer.
BEST SOIL	Loose, rich, well-drained soil.
WHEN TO PLANT	Romaine likes cooler weather, so plant in the early spring or fall; the plants take 65 to 70 days to mature.
HOW TO PLANT	Scatter seeds under ¼-inch of soil; if transplanting from pots or seed trays, plant 12 to 18 inches apart.

QUICK TIPS FOR GROWING ROMAINE	
HOW MUCH TO PLANT	8 to 10 plants per person.
WEEDING	Keep the area free of weeds.
WATERING	Romaine likes a lot of water to make it grow fast.
FERTILIZING	Plenty of fertilizer or compost tea to get the plants growing fast.
PESTS AND DISEASES	Rabbits love romaine; keep them out with netting or fencing. Aphids and caterpillars are also attracted to these plants. Use organic or natural sprays to keep them away.
WHEN TO HARVEST	As soon as it's big enough to use.
HOW TO HARVEST	Pick the outer leaves as you're ready to use them in your smoothies and let the inner leaves grow.
STORAGE	You can store the leaves in a plastic bag with a damp paper towel to ensure they stay moist, but it's best to pick just what you need for your smoothie and let the rest grow.

Spinach

Spinach is another cool season crop that does best grown in spring or fall when the temperatures are lower and the days are shorter. Spinach has one of the darkest-colored leaves and because of this offers a wealth of vitamins and minerals, and it will lend this dark, rich green to your smoothie.

QUICK TIPS FOR GROWING SPINACH	
FAMILY NAME	Chenopodiaceae (goosefoot family).
EDIBLE PARTS	Leaves and stems.
LOCATION	Full sun.
BEST SOIL	Rich soil abundant in nitrogen; pH 6.2-6.9.

QUICK TIPS FOR GROWING SPINACH

WHEN TO PLANT	Low-temperature season. Start sowing indoors in April to July and transplant out every 4 weeks, or it can be direct-seeded as soon as the soil is worked.
HOW TO PLANT.	Can be direct-seeded or transplanted. Plant ¼-inch deep, 1 inch apart, and space 6 to 8 inches apart in rows at least 12 inches apart.
HOW MUCH TO PLANT	10 to 15 plants per person each season.
WEEDING	Keep beds well weeded.
WATERING	Keep soil moist; sprinkling will keep the leaves cooler in warm weather.
CARE	May need a little shade if the weather gets warm. A floating row cover works well.
FERTILIZING	Give spinach plants a nitrogen-rich fertilizer once they are grown, or approximately once every 10 to 14 days.
PESTS AND DISEASES	Aphids, slugs, cabbageworms, and leaf miners are common.
WHEN TO HARVEST	Can be harvested at any size from baby leaves to maturity, which ranges from 40 to 50 days.
HOW TO HARVEST	Cut outer leaves as they grow or at the base of a mature plant.
STORAGE	Spinach does not store well. Wash leaves, dry them in a salad spinner, and place them in a sealed plastic bag or container. Spinach will keep in the refrigerator for a few days.

Watercress

Watercress leaves have a peppery flavor that will add a nice bite to any smoothie in which you use them. It also has vitamins K, C, and A, as well as calcium and iron.

QUICK TIPS FOR GROWING WATERCRESS	
FAMILY NAME	Brassicaceae (mustard or cabbage family).
EDIBLE PARTS	Leaves and stems.
LOCATION	In full sun and partial shade.
BEST SOIL	Rich soil, high in organic content.
WHEN TO PLANT	Early spring.
HOW TO PLANT.	Space the seeds 3 to 4 inches apart. A good environment is to plant the cress in soil-filled pots that are placed in a tray filled with water. If you do this, change the water every three or four days.
HOW MUCH TO PLANT	7 to 8 pots per person.
WEEDING	If you plant in a water tray, this is not a consideration.
WATERING	The water tray mentioned is the best option.
CARE	As long as the plants are not allowed to dry out, watercress doesn't require much care.
FERTILIZING	Watercress in a water tray does not need fertilizer.
PESTS AND DISEASES	Flea beetles and mustard beetles like watercress. To get rid of them, dunk the entire pot under water and hold it there for an hour or so.
WHEN TO HARVEST	Cress germinates in 8 to 12 days; pick when the leaves are fully grown. Be sure to harvest before the plants go to flower, or they will turn bitter.

QUICK TIPS FOR GROWING WATERCRESS	
HOW TO HARVEST	Snap the leaves off at the base of the stem.
STORAGE	Store in a clean plastic bag with a damp paper towel. However, I strongly recommend harvesting only what you need for your smoothie, so you'll get the freshest watercress possible.

Chapter 12
Brassicas and Root Vegetables

Also known as the mustard or cabbage family, brassicas include such favorites as broccoli, Brussels sprouts, cabbage, cauliflower, and kale. They are cold, hardy vegetables that produce a lot of food for the space they use. They grow well in most soil types. Adding shredded leaves to the area where you will be planting the following year will help to produce fabulous brassicas for you.

Root vegetables, on the other hand, are grown for their edible roots. They are generally easy to grow and have similar growing needs and soil conditions. They need a well-prepared garden bed with a light soil to grow their best. Garlic and onions are grown mainly for their roots but have some distinctive characteristics of their own.

Broccoli

Broccoli is a cool season crop and is probably the easiest of all the brassica family to grow. Most varieties will produce one large head averaging about six to eight inches in diameter. Once this head is cut off, the plant will continue to produce side branches with smaller heads. Keep cutting these before they flower and you will be able to harvest broccoli from one plant for several weeks.

Broccoli

The broccoli plant may bolt if the weather gets hot. This means the plant will go to flower more quickly than it normally would in cooler weather. It is best to plant broccoli early in the spring (April) and then again in late summer if you have a mild fall and winter.

✳ *Smoothie Garden Solution*

Broccoli is one of the most popular vegetables for the health-conscious eater. A half cup of cooked broccoli has 75 mg vitamin C, 1,300 IU beta carotene, 3 grams protein, 5 grams dietary fiber, and only 40 calories, making it one of the top ten healthy foods to eat.

Broccoli often does best transplanted. This allows you to start your plants indoors so they get more growth before the heat of the summer arrives.

QUICK TIPS FOR GROWING BROCCOLI

FAMILY NAME	Brassicaceae (mustard or cabbage family).
EDIBLE PARTS	Flower buds and stems.
LOCATION	Cool area.
BEST SOIL	Rich, moist but well-drained, loamy soil; pH 6.0–6.8.
WHEN TO PLANT	Start Indoors April to mid-July, then transplant out after 6 to 8 weeks.
HOW TO PLANT	Space transplants 16 to 24 inches apart in rows spaced 2 to 3 feet apart. Sow seeds ½-inch deep, 4 inches apart, then thin seedlings.
HOW MUCH TO PLANT	10 to 15 plants per person each season.
WEEDING	Keep well weeded around the base of the plant.
WATERING	Water deeply at least once a week around the base of the plant. Hand-watering or drip irrigation are best. If an overhead sprinkler is used, the water is blocked from reaching the roots by the large leaves.
FERTILIZING	Start to fertilize about 3 weeks after setting out the transplants and again when the bud starts to form on the plant.
PESTS AND DISEASES	Root maggots, cabbageworms, and clubroot are common. Crop rotation is essential to prevent pests and diseases.
WHEN TO HARVEST	Broccoli usually matures in 50 to 72 days. Cut the center head when it is about 5 to 6 inches in diameter or before the buds start to open.
HOW TO HARVEST	Cut the center head with about 4 inches of stem using a sharp knife. The plant will form side branches off the main stem, which will produce smaller heads that need to be cut before they flower.
STORAGE	Broccoli will stay for a few weeks in your refrigerator. It is best to put it on ice or into the refrigerator as soon as it is harvested.

Cauliflower

Cauliflower is said to be the most difficult vegetable in the brassica family to grow. It is a cool-season vegetable, but it is also very sensitive to frost. Sunlight will turn the white head a darkish yellow color, so each head needs to be covered or blanched. This vegetable can be time-consuming and not a sure thing for a home gardener, but it is worth a try.

Cauliflower

There are several different varieties of cauliflower, some in bright colors of purple and orange! There are varieties that do not need to be blanched because the leaves grow in a certain way that covers the head and protects it from the sun.

✳ *Smoothie Garden Solution*

What does it mean to blanch a vegetable plant? The sunlight needs to be prevented from reaching the plant in order for it to remain whitish in color. To make this happen, the plant is usually covered with its own leaves. If the white variety of cauliflower is not blanched, the sun may cause it to turn brownish. There are different varieties of cauliflower that are grown for their color; these do not need blanching.

Cauliflower needs a moderately rich soil. When preparing your garden bed, add in several inches of compost or aged animal manure as well as some fertilizer rich in phosphorus. This is a good area of your garden to put shredded leaves; cauliflower will do well with them decomposing in the bed. Cauliflower is also a great vegetable to mulch because the soil needs to be kept moist, especially if there is a long dry spell.

QUICK TIPS FOR GROWING CAULIFLOWER

FAMILY NAME	Brassicaceae (mustard or cabbage family).
EDIBLE PARTS	Heads.
LOCATION	Cool, sunny area.
BEST SOIL	Rich, moist but well-drained, loamy soil; pH 6.0–6.8.
WHEN TO PLANT	Start indoors April to mid-July, then transplant out after 6 to 8 weeks.
HOW TO PLANT	Space transplants 16 to 24 inches apart in rows 2 to 3 feet apart. Sow seeds ½-inch deep, 4 inches apart, then thin seedlings.
HOW MUCH TO PLANT	10 to 15 plants per person each season.
WEEDING	Keep well weeded around the base of the plant.
WATERING	Water deeply at least once a week around the base of the plant. Hand-watering or drip irrigation are best; if an overhead sprinkler is used, the large leaves block the water from the roots.
CARE	Cauliflower heads need to be blanched if you want them to remain a whitish color. Start blanching 3 weeks before you plan to harvest.
FERTILIZING	Start to fertilize about 3 weeks after setting out the transplants and again when the bud starts to form on the plant.
PESTS AND DISEASES	Root maggots, cabbageworms, and clubroot are common. Crop rotation is essential for prevention of pests and diseases.
WHEN TO HARVEST	Cauliflower usually matures in 55 to 100 days.
HOW TO HARVEST	Cut the head of cauliflower off at the base of the plant using a sharp knife.
STORAGE	A head of cauliflower will last for a couple of weeks in the refrigerator. Cauliflower can be frozen and used as you need it.

Kale

Kale has high levels of vitamin C and calcium and the highest levels of beta carotene of all the green vegetables. It is a hardy vegetable. Kale will survive over the winter and the leaves are more tender and sweet once they have been touched by frost. Kale will easily go to seed and spread throughout your garden, so pull the plants out before the seeds spread if you want to contain it.

✳ *Smoothie Garden Solution*

Adding dolomite lime to the garden soil when preparing the beds will help to keep the soil at a good pH for these plants. Lime will also help prevent clubroot and other fungal diseases that brassicas are prone to.

There are several different varieties of kale, which are easily distinguishable because of their color and leaf. The most common are probably the green, curly leaf varieties. Some other varieties are Red Russian, which have gray-green leaves with a purplish stem; Lacinato, which has a dark, blue-green-colored leaf; Redbor, which has dark red leaves; and Improved Siberian, which has flat green leaves.

✳ *Smoothie Garden Solution*

A good garden fork is invaluable. Gently loosen the soil around the area where the plant is growing and then use your hands to pull up the root. Be careful not to pierce your beets or break the carrots when digging them. If you do, use them as soon as possible.

QUICK TIPS FOR GROWING KALE

FAMILY NAME	Brassicaceae (mustard or cabbage family).
EDIBLE PARTS	Leaves and stems.
LOCATION	Cool, sunny area.
BEST SOIL	Rich, well drained; pH 6.5–6.8.
WHEN TO PLANT	Start indoors April to mid-July, then transplant out after 6 to 8 weeks.
HOW TO PLANT	Space transplants 18 to 20 inches apart in rows 2 to 3 feet apart. Sow seeds ¼-inch deep, 2 to 4 inches apart, then thin seedlings.
HOW MUCH TO PLANT	5 to 10 plants per person each season.
COMPANION PLANTS	For a positive effect, plant with beans, onions, potatoes, dill, sage, and oregano. Planting with tomatoes and lettuce will have a negative effect on cauliflower.
WEEDING	Keep well weeded around the base of the plant.
WATERING	Water deeply at least once a week around the base of the plant. Hand-watering or drip irrigation are best; if an overhead sprinkler is used, the large leaves will block the water from the roots.
FERTILIZING	Start to fertilize about 3 weeks after setting out the transplants and regularly until you harvest them.
PESTS AND DISEASES	Root maggots, cabbageworms, and club root are common. Crop rotation is essential for prevention of pests and disease.
WHEN TO HARVEST	Kale usually matures in 55 to 75 days.
HOW TO HARVEST	Cut off leaves as you need them and the plant will keep producing for you all season long. Mature plants can be harvested at the base.
STORAGE	Eat the leaves as soon as possible after harvesting; they lose nutrients when stored. They will stay in the refrigerator for up to 1 week.

Beets

Beets are a love-or-hate vegetable; either you love them or you have no desire to eat them at all. They are a great addition to any home garden because they are easy to grow, have a long harvest, take up a small amount of space in your garden, and can be stored. They have more than one edible part and can be eaten raw or cooked, so they are a very versatile vegetable. The young leaves are used with other baby greens in popular salad mixes. The mature leaves can be steamed for a nutritious side dish to add to any meal. The roots can be harvested as sweet and tender baby beets or they can be left to grow to maturity to be harvested as you need them all summer and fall.

The many variety of beets give you more options than just a round red beet. You can buy seeds that will produce elongated roots, which have a milder taste. Beets can now be grown in a multitude of colors. There are white, yellow, orange, and striped varieties.

✳ Smoothie Garden Solution

Peeling beets can be messy and can stain your hands and cooking area, so leave the peel on. Once the beets are cooked, just plunge them into ice-cold water and the skins will just slip off. If you do get stains on your fingers, rub them with a fresh lemon and the red juice will easily wash off.

Beets like a fairly rich soil that is free of rocks and debris. Add in aged animal manure and lime if needed when preparing your garden bed. Make sure your bed is well prepared with at least a foot of loose-tilled soil for the roots to grow. Remove any lumps, rocks, or sticks from the soil so they don't impede the growth of the root. Beets are usually direct-seeded to your garden bed; however, they are slow to germinate, so mark the bed where they are planted. The seed can produce more than one plant; they will need to be thinned so there is only one plant for every three to four inches of garden soil as the seedlings start to grow.

QUICK TIPS FOR GROWING BEETS

FAMILY NAME	Chenopodiaceae (goosefoot family).
EDIBLE PARTS	Roots and tops.
LOCATION	Sunny, open area.
BEST SOIL	Fertile, well-drained soil, clean bed; pH 6.0–6.8.
WHEN TO PLANT	Sow April to mid-July for a continuous harvest.
HOW TO PLANT	Sow seeds ½-inch deep and 1 inch apart in rows spaced 16 to 24 inches apart. Keep the soil moist until seeds have germinated; this can take from 14 to 21 days. Once seedlings are a couple of inches high, thin them so there is only 1 plant for every 3 inches of soil.
HOW MUCH TO PLANT	10 to 20 feet per person.
WEEDING	Keep well weeded, especially when plants are small.
WATERING	The soil needs to be kept moist when seeds are first planted. Once plants have sprouted, water regularly. If you are using an overhead sprinkler, make sure you leave it on long enough for the water to penetrate several inches to reach the roots.
FERTILIZING	Dig in compost or aged animal manure and a balanced fertilizer when preparing the beds.
PESTS AND DISEASES	Leaf miners, beet webworms, flea beetles, wireworms, and leaf spot can affect your beet plants.
WHEN TO HARVEST	Beets mature in 45 to 65 days. You can start cutting the young leaves for salad when they are about 3 inches high. Start harvesting the roots once they reach the size of a golf ball. Harvest all your beets before the first frost in the fall.
HOW TO HARVEST	Cut the leaves individually or harvest the whole plant by gently tugging it from the ground. Larger beets may require a garden fork to gently loosen the surrounding soil before pulling.
STORAGE	To store, cut off the greens, leaving 2 to 3 inches of stem. The greens can be stored separately for up to a week in a plastic bag in the refrigerator. The roots can be placed in a plastic bag and will keep in the refrigerator for up to 3 weeks. If you have a large amount to store, they can be packed in a box filled with peat moss and stored in a root cellar.

Carrots

Carrots are one of the most popular vegetables in the world. Pulling a baby carrot from the garden, wiping off a little dirt, and biting into it is an experience everyone should have. There is nothing better than a freshly picked carrot! Carrots are great to grow if you have children around because they grow fairly quickly and can be picked at any size—and children love to pull them out of the ground.

The time-consuming part of growing carrots is the bed preparation. Carrots need a deep, loose, sandy soil that is free of debris to grow their best. They are a great vegetable to grow in raised beds because the soil texture is often lighter than in a regular garden bed. If you have a heavy soil, it is important to dig in compost or aged animal manure to lighten the soil; however, if the soil is too fertile the carrots may get hairy and misshapen and they may not taste as good. It can take a few years to get your soil to the proper consistency to grow fabulous carrots. If there are any obstructions in the soil, the carrot will grow around them, producing oddly shaped roots. It is important to take the time to break up any lumps of soil and pick out rocks that are larger than very small pebbles before planting your carrot seeds.

Carrots are a cool-season crop and are best planted in the early spring to be harvested in the summer. If you live in an area where you get mild winters, plant another crop in late summer for a fall harvest. The carrot has its best flavor when grown in the full sun with cool nights. Carrots are direct-seeded and need to be kept moist in order to germinate, so you may have to water the garden bed two to three times a day until they germinate. Water carefully so as not to wash the seeds away. It is important to keep the soil moistened because the seeds may not be able to break through the hard and crusty soil if the soil dries out.

To harvest large carrots so they do not break off, gently push the carrot downward into the ground and then pull it upward. This breaks the roots and makes it easier to pull up.

QUICK TIPS FOR GROWING CARROTS

FAMILY NAME	Umbelliferae or Apiaceae (carrot or parsley family).
EDIBLE PARTS	Roots.
LOCATION	Sunny location.
BEST SOIL	Fertile, sandy, loamy soil, free of debris; pH 5.5–6.8.
WHEN TO PLANT	Sow direct starting in April up to mid-July. Plant a row every few weeks so you will be able to eat carrots all season long.
HOW TO PLANT	Sow seeds ¼-inch deep, ½-inch apart, in rows spaced 12 to 24 inches apart. Seeds can take from 7 to 21 days to germinate and need to be kept moist until then. Once they are a few inches tall, thin them so plants are 2 to 4 inches apart.
HOW MUCH TO PLANT	25 to 30 feet per person each season.
COMPANION PLANTS	Plant with beans, leeks, onions, peas, and radishes.
WEEDING	Carrots need to be kept free of weeds in order to grow well.
WATERING	Water regularly, preferably with a drip irrigation system; carrots grow best if the leaves are not wet.
FERTILIZING	It is best to add compost or manure in the fall to the area where you will be growing your carrots the following spring.
PESTS AND DISEASES	Carrot flies, aphids, leafhoppers, and nematodes are some common pests that affect carrots.
WHEN TO HARVEST	Carrots will mature in 30 to 80 days, depending on whether you want to harvest baby carrots of fully mature ones. You can start harvesting carrots once they are about the size of your finger.
HOW TO HARVEST	Gently pull the carrot out of the ground. For mature carrots, push them gently downward to break the roots, then pull them out. This will prevent them from breaking off underground.
STORAGE	When storing carrots, remove the tops. They will keep in a plastic bag in the refrigerator for several weeks or they can be frozen or canned. If you have a large amount, leave them in the ground covered with several inches of mulch and harvest as needed.

Garlic

Garlic is a cool-season crop grown
mainly for its bulb, although the flower
stem is also edible and very tasty. Garlic
is a fairly hardy vegetable. It needs
a sunny, well-drained area. Garlic is
usually planted in the fall, either in
October or at the latest early November,
and is harvested the following June.

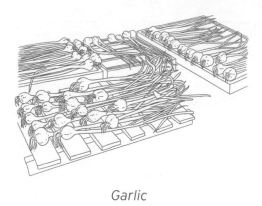

Garlic

Choose the biggest cloves to plant and mulch the beds after they are planted.
Garlic will grow slowly over the winter and will shoot up quickly once the days
start to get longer in January and February. In the spring, keep the plants well
weeded and give them more mulch and regular watering if you do not get any
rain. In early spring, the garlic plants will produce flower stalks, which are called
garlic scapes. They can be eaten like garlic cloves. Removing the stem before it
fully flowers will allow the plant to put more energy into producing a larger bulb.

✳ *Smoothie Garden Solution*

Garlic has been renowned for its powerful medicinal qualities for centuries.
Hieroglyphs of garlic were engraved on the Great Pyramid of Giza to protect
the builders. Doctors in ancient Greece and Rome believed garlic was a cure-
all for many ailments and diseases. Today, people consume garlic and garlic
supplements for their antioxidants.

The garlic bulbs are ready to be harvested once the garlic tops start to turn
brown and die back. When harvesting your garlic, use a garden fork to loosen
the soil so the bulbs do not break off. Garlic needs to be dried in order for it to
keep properly; leave the bulbs in the sun to cure for up to three weeks. Protect
them from the rain by covering them or bringing them indoors in bad weather.

QUICK TIPS FOR GROWING GARLIC	
FAMILY NAME	Alliaceae (onion family).
EDIBLE PARTS	Bulb (cloves) and flower stem.
LOCATION	Sunny, dry area.
BEST SOIL	Rich, well-drained soil; pH 6.0–6.8.
WHEN TO PLANT	Plant bulbs in the fall if you live in a warmer climate or in the early spring if you live in an extremely cold climate where the ground freezes in early fall.
HOW TO PLANT	Set out cloves of garlic 2 inches deep, 6 to 8 inches apart in rows spaced 16 to 24 inches apart. Plant the cloves with the pointed end up.
HOW MUCH TO PLANT	5 to 10 feet per person.
COMPANION PLANTS	For a positive effect, plant near carrots and tomatoes. Beans, peas, and strawberries can have a negative effect, so avoid planting them near garlic.
WEEDING	Keep well weeded.
WATERING	Needs regular watering in the spring if there is very little rainfall.
CARE	Mulch with straw or hay in the fall and again in the spring when the plants are 1 foot high to prevent weeds and keep the soil from drying out.
FERTILIZING	Fertilize with compost tea or fish fertilizer after the flower stalks have started to form.
PESTS AND DISEASES	Aphids and thrips can be a problem. Using crop rotation will prevent most pests and disease.
WHEN TO HARVEST	Garlic takes 6 to 10 months to fully mature. When the tops start to turn brown and die back, garlic is ready to be harvested.
HOW TO HARVEST	Loosen the soil around your plants with a garden fork and then gently pull out the bulbs, trying to keep the stem and bulb intact. The bulb will dry better if it is not broken off.

QUICK TIPS FOR GROWING GARLIC	
STORAGE	If dried and stored properly, garlic will keep for several months. Once cured in the sun for a few weeks, clean off any dirt remaining on the bulb and store it in a paper bag or box in a cool, dry storage area. Garlic can be braided and hung in a cool, dark area.

Green Onions

Green onions, also known as scallions or spring onions, are immature onions that are harvested before the bulb fully develops. Their taste is milder than mature onions, perfect for your smoothie. If you want to add some color, add purple or red varieties of scallions to your Green Smoothie Garden.

QUICK TIPS FOR GROWING GREEN ONIONS	
FAMILY NAME	Alliaceae (onion family).
EDIBLE PARTS	All.
LOCATION	Full sun.
BEST SOIL	Rich, well-drained soil, pH 6.0–7.5
WHEN TO PLANT	Early spring, as soon as the soil can be worked. In Zone 7 and above, plant in September for a winter harvest.
HOW TO PLANT	Start them indoors and plant the seedlings 1 to 1¼-inches apart. You can also plant from roots. Cut off the onion about 1 inch above the root and plant the root in your garden.
HOW MUCH TO PLANT	10 to 15 per person.
WEEDING	Keep the area weed free.
WATERING	Once sprouted, green onions need about 1 inch of water per week. Don't let the soil get soggy.

QUICK TIPS FOR GROWING GREEN ONIONS

CARE	Green onions are pretty low maintenance. Make sure the soil is fed regularly with compost tea and kept free of weeds. For best results, rotate them regularly around the garden each year.
FERTILIZING	Put in plenty of compost when first planting, and feed regularly with compost tea or other natural fertilizers.
PESTS AND DISEASES	Discourage aphids and caterpillars with natural sprays.
WHEN TO HARVEST	Any time after the onions reach 6 inches or more in height.
HOW TO HARVEST	With a sharp knife, cut off the onion about 1 inch above the root; the onion will resprout.
STORAGE	Green onions can be stored for several days in a plastic bag with a damp paper towel, but they'll taste best in your smoothie if you use them immediately upon harvesting.

Chapter 13
Peppers, Herbs, and Others

Peppers

Peppers come in various shapes, from chunky to long and skinny and round to conical. You'll find them in shades of green, red, and yellow. Their flavors range from mild and sweet to sizzling hot. Sweet peppers are also known as bell peppers because of the shape of the fruit. They are often harvested when green; that way, the plant produces more fruit. When left on the plant to mature, bell peppers will turn either yellow,

Bell peppers

orange, or red depending on the variety. Hot pepper plants grow taller and have narrower leaves than the bell varieties and their fruit can range in size from about one to seven inches long.

Peppers are a little touchy to grow. They need lots of full sun, warm daytime temperatures, cool nighttime temperatures, fertile soil, and lots of water. Sweet peppers need a little less heat than hot pepper varieties. When preparing your garden bed, add compost or aged animal manure. Peppers can then be seeded directly if you have a long growing season; however, they often do better started indoors in early spring and transplanted out once the temperature reaches 65ºF.

❋ Smoothie Garden Solution

Transplant your vegetables on a cloudy day or later in the day when the sun is not so hot. The hot sun can wilt or scorch the young leaves, leaving them stressed. Make sure the transplants are moist before you plant them and gently water them after they have been placed in the ground. Watering the plant will help the roots become established.

Peppers are a very popular vegetable, either cooked by themselves or with other foods. They are also eaten raw in salads or as appetizers. When preparing to use your pepper, cut it in half, remove the stem, and rinse away the seeds. Fresh or dried hot peppers need to be handled carefully because the oils in the skin can burn your skin or eyes. It is suggested that you use rubber gloves and hold the hot pepper under water when preparing it. Remove the seeds from a hot pepper if you want to cut down the heat; the seeds add to the hot taste.

QUICK TIPS FOR GROWING PEPPERS	
FAMILY NAME	Solanaceae (nightshade family).
EDIBLE PARTS	Fruits.
LOCATION	Very sunny area.
BEST SOIL	Fertile, well-drained soil that does not have an excess of nitrogen; soil that is too rich will form leaves but poor fruiting; pH 5.5-6.8.
WHEN TO PLANT	Sow seeds indoors 6 to 8 weeks before you plan to put them into your garden. Transplant them when the temperature is 65°F.
HOW TO PLANT	Set out plants 18 inches apart in rows spaced 30 to 36 inches apart.
HOW MUCH TO PLANT	5 to 10 plants per person.
WEEDING	Keep well weeded when plants are small.

QUICK TIPS FOR GROWING PEPPERS

WATERING	Water regularly and keep soil moist when the plant is flowering and fruiting.
FERTILIZING	Use fish fertilizer or compost tea after the first bloom and then after the fruit starts to form.
PESTS AND DISEASES	Aphids, armyworms, Colorado potato beetles, corn borers, mites, and cutworms are some common pests.
WHEN TO HARVEST	Peppers mature between 60 and 95 days after planting depending on the variety. Harvest sweet peppers when they are firm and full size. You can harvest them when they are green or leave them to turn red, orange, or yellow. Harvest hot peppers when they are full size and have turned yellow, red, or dark green depending on the variety.
HOW TO HARVEST	Cut or gently pull the pepper from the plant, leaving a stem of ½-inch.
STORAGE	Fresh peppers will last 1 to 2 weeks in the refrigerator if not washed, and placed in a sealed plastic bag. Peppers can be frozen, dried, and preserved by pickling or canning them.

✲ *Smoothie Garden Solution*

The secret to a healthy pepper with good color and flavor is adequate water and fertilizer. The pepper plant does not need a lot of nitrogen; this will promote leaf growth but not fruits. Keep the plants mulched with grass clippings to keep the soil moist and free of weeds.

Basil

Basil is a bushy plant that can grow up to eighteen inches high if you treat it well. There are a wide variety of types of this herb, including lemon, fine-leaf, purple, and cinnamon. Basil is a common component of Italian dishes, but it can lend a distinctive flavor to your smoothies as well.

QUICK TIPS FOR GROWING BASIL	
FAMILY NAME	Lamiaceae (mint family).
EDIBLE PARTS	Leaves.
LOCATION	Full sun.
BEST SOIL	Rich, well-drained soil, with some compost mixed in.
WHEN TO PLANT	Best to be started indoors in early spring and transplanted outdoors once the soil is warm, usually late May.
HOW TO PLANT	Transplant 6 to 8 inches apart.
HOW MUCH TO PLANT	1 to 2 plants per person.
WEEDING	Keep weed free.
WATERING	Basil likes regular water, but not to excess. Watering every day is fine in hot weather, but in normal weather every other day is fine.
CARE	Pinch off the plant's upper leaves to encourage bushiness. Avoid letting the basil go to seed.
FERTILIZING	Fertilize the soil about once a month with compost tea.
PESTS AND DISEASES	Cutworms, aphid, and spider mites. To keep your soil fertile, mulch to keep weeds down, water properly, and hand-pick if you see the pests.
WHEN TO HARVEST	When the plant is at least 8 inches.
HOW TO HARVEST	Snap off the leaves close to the stem.
STORAGE	Store in a plastic bag for several days, but whenever possible use the fresh leaves in your green smoothie.

Cilantro

Cilantro is also sometimes referred to as coriander leaf or Chinese parsley. Its seeds are called coriander. It's a versatile herb used in many recipes, and adds a delicious touch to many smoothies. If your plant seems big, don't worry; you'll find plenty of other uses for it in the kitchen. At the end of the season, cut a big bunch, tie it with string, and hang it in a warm, dry place for several weeks before crumbling the leaves into an herb jar.

The biggest challenge to growing cilantro is that it doesn't like hot weather and will go to seed if the weather gets too warm.

QUICK TIPS FOR GROWING CILANTRO	
FAMILY NAME	Apiaceae (carrot or parsley family).
EDIBLE PARTS	Leaves and stems.
LOCATION	Full sun or partial shade.
BEST SOIL	Rich, loose, well-drained soil.
WHEN TO PLANT	Successive plantings every 2 to 3 weeks from early September through February.
HOW TO PLANT	Sow beneath ½-inch of soil, thinning to 12 inches between plants.
HOW MUCH TO PLANT	1 to 2 plants per person.
WEEDING	Keep weed free.
WATERING	Cilantro likes regular watering, but be sure not to overwater.
CARE	Cilantro likes cool nights and sunny (but not hot) days. It can withstand frosts quite well.
FERTILIZING	Composted soil at the beginning is best, together with doses of compost tea, fish emulsion, and seaweed.
PESTS AND DISEASES	Most bugs are apparently repelled by cilantro's smell, although ladybugs and butterflies make frequent visits.

QUICK TIPS FOR GROWING CILANTRO	
WHEN TO HARVEST	When the plant is at least 6 inches.
HOW TO HARVEST	Cut or snap the base of the stems at the outer parts of the plant.
STORAGE	Store in a plastic bag for several days, but whenever possible use the fresh leaves in your green smoothie.

✳ *Smoothie Garden Solution*

As soon as the weather gets much over 75°F, cilantro will "bolt"—that is, start to flower prematurely. Let it go to seed and keep the area around the plant clear of weeds. The following year, you'll see little cilantro plants making their way into the sun. You can turn that corner of your garden into a cilantro paradise.

Mint

Mint is versatile, easy to grow, and easy to care for. You can use it to give a wonderful, fresh taste to your smoothies, as well as making fresh mint tea, mint ice cream, and many more amazing recipes. There are a variety of mint flavors available from garden centers, so pick the one that most appeals to you.

QUICK TIPS FOR GROWING MINT	
FAMILY NAME	Lamiaceae (mint family).
EDIBLE PARTS	Leaves.
LOCATION	Morning sun and afternoon shade. Mint tends to spread, so give it some room to grow.
BEST SOIL	Rich, moist soil.
WHEN TO PLANT	Early spring after the last frost.
HOW TO PLANT	Mint is challenging to grow from seed; it's best to start it from an existing plant or purchase a healthy transplant.
HOW MUCH TO PLANT	1 plant per person.
WEEDING	Keep the area weed free.
WATERING	Mint likes a lot of moisture, so water regularly and make sure the area doesn't dry out.
CARE	One of the biggest challenges with mint is to make sure it doesn't spread to the point that it chokes out other plants. Keep a careful eye on its root system and trim where necessary. It is best to grow mint in a large pot so it does not spread throughout your garden.
FERTILIZING	Mint will grow in most soils; once a year mulch around the base of the plant with compost or aged manure and your plant will be happy.

QUICK TIPS FOR GROWING MINT	
PESTS AND DISEASES	Mint is usually pest free.
WHEN TO HARVEST	When plant stems are at least 6 inches in height.
HOW TO HARVEST	Snip off leaves as necessary.
STORAGE	Mint leaves can be stored fresh in plastic with a damp towel for several days or can be dried and crumbled. For the freshest, mintiest taste for your smoothie, use the leaves as soon as you pick them.

Parsley

Parsley is one of those ubiquitous herbs that seems to have been part of our food forever. Even in the culinary wasteland of the 1950s and 1960s, you couldn't go to a restaurant without the entrée coming to the table with a bit of curly-leaf parsley on the plate—just to give it some class.

What was only recognized more recently is that the flavor of parsley is an important addition to many dishes, and as well to many of your favorite smoothies. Fortunately, it's easy to grow and, given the right conditions, returns year after year. It's also a valuable source of vitamins A and C as well as calcium and iron. While some people use curly-leaf parsley for garnish, most prefer flat-leaf (sometimes called Italian) parsley for its flavor.

QUICK TIPS FOR GROWING PARSLEY	
FAMILY NAME	Umbelliferae or Apiaceae (carrot or parsley family).
EDIBLE PARTS	Leaves and stems.
LOCATION	Sun with afternoon shade.
BEST SOIL	Rich, moist soil.

QUICK TIPS FOR GROWING PARSLEY

WHEN TO PLANT	Start the seeds indoors the first week of March. Plant outside when the weather has started to turn warmer (although parsley can handle a frost–just not too much).
HOW TO PLANT	In seeding trays. When transplanting, leave about 12 inches between the plants.
HOW MUCH TO PLANT	1 to 2 plants per person.
WEEDING	Keep the area weed free.
WATERING	Parsley likes moist soil, so water frequently.
CARE	Parsley needs a lot of water, especially during the height of summer.
FERTILIZING	Dig in compost before planting; mulch with straw and fertilize with liquid fish emulsion.
PESTS AND DISEASES	Parsleyworm. Handpicking is the best prevention.
WHEN TO HARVEST	When the stems are at least 6 inches long.
HOW TO HARVEST	Using a sharp knife, cut stems from the outside of the plant just above the ground; trim off the stems before using.
STORAGE	Store in a plastic bag with a damp towel for several days, but you'll get the best flavor for your smoothies if you use parsley the same day you harvest it.

Celery

Celery needs a three- to four-month growing season. It requires cool weather and likes a fairly consistent temperature through its growing season. Because of this, it can be a difficult plant for a backyard garden. If you really like eating celery, give it a try. It may need more of your attention, but it will be worth it in the end.

When preparing the celery bed, dig in at least twelve inches of compost or aged manure. To do this, dig a trench about a foot deep and fill it with your compost or manure. This gives you a nice deep bed in which to plant your celery transplants.

To get the stalks to remain light green like you see in the supermarket they will need to be blanched. If celery is not blanched the outer stalks can get brown spots and may become tough. This will give the stalks a milder flavor as well. About three to four weeks before you plan to harvest, tie the tops of the stalks together and mound soil around the plants to prevent the light from reaching them. You can also place a large coffee can with both ends removed around the whole plant.

QUICK TIPS FOR GROWING CELERY	
FAMILY NAME	Umbelliferae or Apiaceae (carrot or parsley family).
EDIBLE PARTS	Stalk and root.
LOCATION	Level, open area.
BEST SOIL	Celery is a heavy feeder and needs a rich, well-drained soil; pH 6.0-7.0.
WHEN TO PLANT	Start seedlings indoors in late February to April; transplant out in late spring when plants are about 4 or 5 inches tall.
HOW TO PLANT	Celery can be transplanted or direct-seeded. Space the plants 8 inches apart in rows at least 12 inches apart.
HOW MUCH TO PLANT	5 to 10 plants per person.

QUICK TIPS FOR GROWING CELERY	
COMPANION PLANTS	For a positive effect, plant with beans, brassicas, spinach, squash, tomatoes, and cucumbers. Stay away from carrots and parsnips.
WEEDING	Keep well weeded.
WATERING	Needs heavy watering, so keep soil moist.
CARE	Blanch for best flavor and to get whitish stalks.
FERTILIZING	Put compost around the base of the plant 3 weeks after planting and then again after 6 weeks after planting.
PESTS AND DISEASES	Aphids, cabbage loopers, leafhoppers, damping off, and mildew.
WHEN TO HARVEST	Takes 90 to 110 days to mature.
HOW TO HARVEST	Cut individual stalks as you need them or cut the whole bunch off at the base.
STORAGE	Will not store long once harvested. If you live in an area with mild winters, celery can be left in the garden over winter and harvested as needed.

✳ *Smoothie Garden Solution*

To make limp celery crispy again, cut off the end of the stalk and stand it upright in a jar or vase of cold water. Place it in your refrigerator and leave it in the water until it becomes crispy again. Then store it in a sealed plastic bag or airtight container in the refrigerator.

Cucumbers

There are a wide variety of cucumbers to choose from. They are easy to grow, so cucumbers are a great choice for any gardener. They are a perfect vegetable for growing in containers. The three most common types of cucumbers are the long English varieties, which have an edible peel; the slicing varieties, which have a harder peel that is usually not eaten; and small cucumbers used for pickling. Cucumbers are a climbing vegetable plant; they do best if grown on a trellis. This allows air to circulate around the plant and light to reach the fruit, which will help to prevent pests and diseases. If the fruit is touching the ground, it will often rot before it matures.

Cucumbers

When preparing your garden bed, add two to three inches of compost or aged animal manure, as this vegetable needs a fertile soil to grow its best. Cucumber seeds need a warm soil to germinate, so they are often started indoors and then transplanted out once the weather warms up. This is especially important if you live in a cooler climate. Cucumber plants grow quickly and can be harvested at various sizes depending on the variety. The fruit needs to be picked regularly so more will grow.

✳ *Smoothie Garden Solution*

Some people complain of bitter-tasting cucumbers. To grow tasty, nonbitter cucumbers, you need to have a soil that is not too acidic, so add lime to your garden bed in the spring. Inconsistent watering or large temperature differences can stress the plant, which can also cause the bitter taste. To avoid this, water regularly and protect the plant from the cold.

Cucumbers need to be pollinated, so it is important to know if the variety you choose is a hybrid or standard. Standard varieties have both male and female flowers on the same vine; insects or the wind will do the pollinating for you. The male flower comes out first and looks like a miniature cucumber. The female flower is identified by a swollen ovary just behind the male flower. Hybrid varieties have separate female and male plants and will need to be pollinated by hand. If you have saved cucumber seeds from the past or a friend has given them to you and you are not sure of the variety, check the plant as it grows to see what kind of flowers it is producing. If there is only a male or female flower, no fruit will form. Go to your garden center and purchase another plant that will pollinate the first one for you.

QUICK TIPS FOR GROWING CUCUMBER	
FAMILY NAME	Cucurbitaceae (gourd family).
EDIBLE PARTS	Fruit.
LOCATION	Cucumbers are great veggies for growing in greenhouses or containers.
BEST SOIL	Rich, warm, well-drained, sandy soil; pH 5.5–6.8
WHEN TO PLANT	Plant in the spring once the soil temperature reaches 60°F.
HOW TO PLANT	Can be direct-seeded or transplanted. Sow seeds 1 inch deep, 6 inches apart in rows 4 to 6 feet apart. This is the best way if you are trellising the cucumber plant.
HOW MUCH TO PLANT	5 to 20 feet per person depending on whether you are going to be pickling any of them.
COMPANION PLANTS	Plant with beans, broccoli, cabbage, lettuce, peas, radishes, and tomatoes. Sage can have a negative effect on cucumber plants, so keep them apart.
WEEDING	Keep well weeded, especially when the plants are small.

QUICK TIPS FOR GROWING CUCUMBER

WATERING	Cucumbers need lots of water. Deep watering at the roots is better than using a sprinkler. If the weather is warm, water the plants every second day, especially if they are growing in a greenhouse or container.
CARE	Cucumbers are best grown on a trellis so the plant gets good air circulation and light.
FERTILIZING	Fertilize with manure tea or fish fertilizer 1 week after the plant blooms and then again 3 weeks later.
PESTS AND DISEASES	Aphids, cucumber beetles, flea beetles, mites, squash bugs, downy mildew, and powdery mildew can all affect the cucumber plant. Make sure you do not compost diseased plants!
WHEN TO HARVEST	Harvest the fruit when it is 6 to 12 inches long; this may vary depending on the variety. The cucumber will keep longer if harvested in the early morning when it is cooler. Pick the fruit regularly so that new fruit will keep forming.
HOW TO HARVEST	Cut the fruit from the plant rather than twisting or pulling it off, which can damage the plant.
STORAGE	Cucumbers are best wrapped in plastic and stored in the refrigerator. They will keep for up to 1 week.

Peas

Peas are a cool-weather vegetable. They do best
when planted in the early spring; if you live in a
climate that has mild winters, do a second planting
in mid-August for a fall harvest. They can withstand
a little frost. Peas like a rich, well-drained soil that
is not too high in nitrogen. They like organic matter, so mix in several inches of
compost or aged animal manure when preparing the garden bed.

Peas

There are three different types of peas. Shelling peas are grown for the
seeds. Snow peas have a flat edible pod and are often used in stir-fries. Snap
peas have an edible pod and seeds that are eaten together. There are several
varieties within each of these types of peas. Some peas will need to be staked;
snow peas and snap peas can grow up to five feet high.

✳ *Smoothie Garden Solution*

Using slender tree branches to support your pea plants as they grow adds
a decorative touch to your garden. Stick several branches firmly into the
ground in a circle, leaning them inward toward each other. Plant six seeds
around the base of each branch. For best support, the branches should be
approximately five feet high with one foot stuck into the ground.

Peas need moisture to germinate, and they often germinate faster if the seed
is soaked overnight. Because peas are planted in the spring, it is important that
the seed and plants do not get waterlogged, or they will most likely rot.

QUICK TIPS FOR GROWING PEAS	
FAMILY NAME	Papilionaceae (legume, pea or bean family).
EDIBLE PARTS	Pods and seeds.
LOCATION	Partial shade.

QUICK TIPS FOR GROWING PEAS	
BEST SOIL	Light, sandy, loamy soil, not too rich in nitrogen; pH 5.5-6.8.
WHEN TO PLANT	Requires moderate temperatures. Direct-seed in early spring as soon as your soil can be worked for an early summer harvest. For a fall harvest, plant in mid-August.
HOW TO PLANT	Sow seeds 1 to 2 inches deep, 1 inch apart in rows 18 to 24 inches apart.
HOW MUCH TO PLANT	50 to 100 feet per person.
COMPANION PLANTS	For a positive effect plant with carrots, corn, cucumbers, eggplants, lettuce, radishes, and spinach. Plants that will have a negative effect are tomatoes, turnips, and rutabagas.
WEEDING	Keep well weeded, especially while the plants are young.
WATERING	Peas require regular watering.
CARE	Put in stakes at the time of planting. They do not do well in the heat, so they may need some shelter once the warm weather comes.
FERTILIZING	Fertilize with fish fertilizer or compost tea after the first heavy bloom and again once the pods start to form.
PESTS AND DISEASES	Use crop rotation to prevent pest and diseases. Aphids, cucumber beetles, and powdery mildew can cause problems.
WHEN TO HARVEST	Depending on the variety, peas will usually mature in 55 to 70 days. Pods need to be picked every few days so the plant knows to produce more. If the pods are not picked, the plant will stop producing. Shelling peas: harvest when pods are full, usually at about 2 to 3 inches long. Snow peas: harvest when the pods are still flat and about 3 inches long. Snap peas: harvest when pods are full and about 2 to 3 inches long.
HOW TO HARVEST	Gently pull the pod from the plant.
STORAGE	Fresh peas will store in the refrigerator for up to 1 week. Peas can be frozen and kept in the freezer for several months. They can be dried and used for future plantings.

Zucchini

Zucchini summer squash needs to be harvested regularly, starting when the squash is 4 to 8 inches long. Tiny zucchini are a delicacy for many chefs and will add a wonderful note to your smoothies. They are tender and taste best when small. They can grow several inches overnight, so check them every few days. If you happen to miss one and it grows too large, harvest it anyway so the plant will produce more.

Zucchini flowers

QUICK TIPS FOR GROWING ZUCCHINI	
FAMILY NAME	Cucurbitaceae (gourd family).
EDIBLE PARTS	Fruits and some seeds.
LOCATION	Sunny area.
BEST SOIL	Fertile, well-drained, light soil. If you have clay soil, add lots of organic matter to lighten it; pH 5.5-6.8.
WHEN TO PLANT	Sow seeds directly when the soil temperature is 60°F. You can start transplants in April and transplant them out approximately 6 weeks later, making sure the soil temperature is warm enough.
HOW TO PLANT	Sow seeds 2 to 3 inches deep, 16 inches apart in rows 3 to 5 feet apart.
HOW MUCH TO PLANT	1 to 2 plants for the family.
WEEDING	Keep well weeded when the plant is young.
WATERING	Zucchini requires regular watering. Watering at the base of the plant rather than overhead is better for the plant.
CARE	Plants need a large amount of space to grow.

QUICK TIPS FOR GROWING ZUCCHINI	
FERTILIZING	Give the plants fish fertilizer or compost tea once they have reached about 1 foot tall and are just starting to spread.
PESTS AND DISEASES	Aphids, cucumber beetles, mites, nematodes, squash bugs, squash vine borers, and powdery mildew can affect zucchini plants.
WHEN TO HARVEST	Zucchini will mature in 50 to 65 days. Harvest once fruits start to form and pick every few days when the fruit is still fairly small (6 to 8 inches); they are tastier when young.
HOW TO HARVEST	Cut from the plant, leaving a small stem on each fruit.
STORAGE	Summer squash will store for up to 1 week in the refrigerator. But for best results, use them in your smoothies right after picking.

Chapter 14
Troubleshooting Your Smoothie Garden

There are so many different problems that can occur in the vegetable garden. You have control over some, such as soil conditions or plant damage. Others, such as the weather or the amount of sunlight your garden gets, are often out of your control. You must become a plant detective to identify the problem and find a solution. This chapter gives you advice and tips on how to identify and treat common problems in your smoothie vegetable garden.

Identify the Problem

Some problems may affect your entire garden while others may affect only one type or one variety of vegetable. Plants are as different as people; some are more susceptible to problems than others. Identifying the problem can take some effort; often, the symptoms of a disease or a pest infestation are similar to those of an undernourished or underwatered plant.

Walk through your smoothie garden and observe your plants every day or once every few days. It's often easier to treat a problem you spot in the early stages before it can spread to other plants or areas of your garden. Before you make a diagnosis, inspect the leaves, blossoms, stems, roots, and surrounding soil. Look for any wilting, distortion, discoloration, holes, eggs, spots, and insects on the leaves. Check the blossoms and fruit for any discoloration, holes, spots, premature dropping, lack of fruiting, and insects or eggs. Study the stems at soil level or slightly below the soil to look for growths such as cankers or galls, wilting, stunted or spindly growth, sticky coating, and eggs or insects on the stem or in the soil around the base of the plant. This information will help you determine if there are any pests on the plant or in the immediate area.

✳ *Smoothie Garden Solution*

Attracting birds to your garden can be one way to keep the unwanted pests under control. Provide a home for birds by placing a birdhouse in a nearby tree. Offer pools of water at ground level for the birds to play in. They do not like their baths too deep; one inch of water is sufficient.

If you have a pest problem in your vegetable garden, it can often be handled by handpicking, trapping insects, or spraying plants with organic remedies. Removing an infected plant can also stop the spread of a disease. If the plant is very diseased, pull it and check the roots for discoloration, decay, eggs, distortions, and insects. Always place diseased plants into a garbage bag as soon as you pull them. This will help keep the problem from spreading throughout your whole garden.

Garden Concerns

So what do you do if you cannot see any pests or specific disease patterns? What else could the problem be?

The most common problems in a vegetable garden are often caused by:

- Overwatering

- Underwatering

- Inadequate nutrients in the soil

- Poor drainage

- Poor air circulation

If a plant is stressed by under- or overwatering or lack of nutrients, it will be more susceptible to pests and disease. Trying to combat the problem early is the best plan of action. Plants are great at letting us know there is a problem. The following section details some common concerns and what you can do in your garden planning and plant maintenance to help the situation.

Standing Rainwater

This means the water is not able to penetrate into the soil. This could be caused by poor soil structure or a hard clay soil. A short-term solution is to hoe the garden area just before a rain to break up the hard surface. This will allow the water to be absorbed more easily into the soil. In the fall or spring, add in more compost or aged animal manure to improve the soil. Doing this every year is a long-term solution to a poor drainage problem.

✳ *Smoothie Garden Solution*

Water is heavier than you think! When watering by hand, make sure you use a lightweight plastic watering container. A two-gallon watering container will weigh up to sixteen pounds when filled with water. That's why it is important to have your water source nearby.

Seeds That Won't Germinate

First, check to see if the seeds are still in the ground. A pest that you cannot see may be eating your seeds or they may be rotting. Soil temperatures that are too low or too high can cause poor or slow seed germination. Make sure you are planting the seed at the recommended time of year and at the recommended depth. Check the seed packet for the proper planting depth and replant. If your seed is old, it may not be viable and you may have to buy some new seeds.

Unhealthy Plants and Stunted Growth

Many factors can be responsible for plants that don't look as healthy as they should or are not growing as well as they should. Low soil fertility or low pH is probably the most common reason. Give the plants a boost with a side dressing of compost or a manure or compost tea. Observe what happens over the next few weeks.

Other causes include lack of sunlight, too little or too much water, and poor drainage. Most vegetable plants need at least six hours of sunlight each day and an inch of water every week. If nature isn't cooperating, you may have to step in yourself.

✳ *Smoothie Garden Solution*

Wood ash is a quick fix for acidic soil. It will neutralize the soil in a few weeks, whereas limestone can take up to six months to do the same job. It is important to thoroughly till the wood ash into the soil in the fall. Use one and a quarter pounds of wood ash for every one pound of lime recommended.

If you are a novice gardener, be patient with yourself. It takes practice and a lot of knowledge to diagnose a problem in your garden. It is often a process of trial and error, even for a seasoned gardener. Having healthy, fertile garden soil goes a long way to having healthy vegetable plants, so concentrate your energy there if you're in doubt.

Signs of Nutrient Deficiency in the Soil

Vegetable plants need fertile soil to grow well. The three main nutrients your vegetable plants need are nitrogen, phosphorus, and potassium. The following table identifies nine additional micronutrients your vegetable plants need. Problems with your vegetable plants can alert you and help you identify soil deficiencies and other concerns.

NUTRIENT DEFICIENCY GUIDE

NUTRIENT	SYMPTOMS	CAUSES	SOLUTIONS
NITROGEN	Plant leaves are light green or yellowish in color.	Easily leaches from the soil.	Mulch or plant a cover crop.
PHOSPHORUS	Plants are stunted and have a purplish color.	Wet, cold soil; low pH (acidic soil).	Plan to lime next spring.
POTASSIUM	Leaves are brown and curling.	Excessive leaching.	Mulch or plant a green manure.
CALCIUM	Stunted plants, stubby roots, and blossom-end rot on tomatoes.	Very acidic soil, excessive dry or wet soil, too-high potassium levels.	Add lime, check for drainage problems, and fertilize carefully.
MAGNESIUM	Yellowish color on older leaves.	Very acidic soil, potassium levels too high.	Add lime and fertilize carefully.
SULFUR	Yellowish color in young leaves and stunted growth.	Low organic matter often found in sandy soil.	Add in compost and aged animal manures in the fall and spring.
BORON	Leaves are distorted, crown of the plant dies.	Soil pH above 6.8 or below 5.5, low organic matter, sandy soil.	Do a soil pH test to see if you need to add in lime or sulfur.
COPPER	Yellowish leaves that become thin and elongated.	High pH (too alkaline).	Add sulfur to the soil in the spring to lower the pH.
IRON	Youngest leaves are light green- or yellow-colored.	High pH (too alkaline), low organic matter, and excessive phosphorus in the soil.	Add sulfur, compost, and aged animal manures in the spring and fall.
ZINC	Yellow beet leaves, rust spots on beans.	High pH (too alkaline), cool wet soil in the spring, and excessive phosphorus in the soil.	Add sulfur and fertilize carefully.
MANGANESE	Mottled yellowish areas on younger leaves.	High pH (too alkaline).	Add sulfur in the spring.
MOLYBDENUM	Distorted leaves, curling at leaf edges, yellowish outer leaves.	Low pH (acidic soil).	Add lime in the spring.

A soil test can tell you the soil pH and reveal any nutrient deficiencies. The soil test will give you an idea of what nutrients are needed and how much to add to your soil to raise them to an optimum level. If you do not want to incur the expense of a soil test, closely observe your vegetable plants for indications of what they may be missing. Note the problem in your journal so you can plan to make the necessary changes or additions to your garden beds next season.

✳ *Smoothie Garden Solution*

Calcium in your soil is essential for growing crunchy cucumbers. Side-dress your cucumber plants with bone meal, gypsum, rock phosphate, or dolomite lime to add in calcium. Pick the cucumbers young; the older they get, the less crunchy they are.

If you observe your plants regularly, you'll be able to tell when there's something wrong. Adding in amendments, fertilizers, or compost teas can easily correct worrying symptoms in your vegetable plants.

What's Wrong with My Plants?

The following table will help you identify what could be causing problems with your vegetable plants and offers some solutions.

Your vegetable plants hold a wealth of information about problems in the garden. They will wilt if they get too much heat or not enough water, they will turn yellow if they are not getting the nutrients they need, and they may even die if they are not taken care of properly. It takes time and knowledge to be able to read your plants and to make a diagnosis based on what you see. Over time, you will get to know your soil conditions and the natural rhythm of your garden, which will make it easier to pinpoint problems and come up with solutions.

PLANT PROBLEM GUIDE

SYMPTOMS	POSSIBLE CAUSES	POSSIBLE CURES
Stunted plants with a yellowish or pale color.	Low fertility, low pH, poor drainage, insects.	Do a soil test for fertility recommendations, add lime, and add in organic matter.
Stunted plants with a purplish color.	Low temperature, lack of phosphorus.	Plant at the recommended temperature and add phosphorus to the soil.
Holes in leaves.	Insects.	Identify the insect by looking on the leaves and use appropriate controls.
Wilting plants.	Dry soil, excess water, and disease.	Irrigate if dry, drain if wet; plant resistant varieties.
Weak, spindling plants.	Too much shade, too much water, too much nitrogen in the soil, planting is too thick.	Place in a sunnier location, avoid excess fertilization, thin plants to proper spacing.
Fruit not forming.	High temperature, low temperature, too much nitrogen, insects.	Plant at the recommended times, avoid overfertilization, identify insects and find the appropriate control.
Abnormal leaves.	Virus disease.	Remove infected leaves.
Spots, molds on stems and leaves.	Disease.	Identify and use appropriate controls.

✳ Smoothie Garden Solution

Many vegetables are related to common weeds, so a diseased weed can spread the sickness to your vegetable plants. Mosaic virus on cucumbers is often spread by milkweed, pokeweed, or ground cherry. Horsenettle and jimsonweed can spread diseases to the nightshade family.

Every garden is different, so what may work for one gardener may not have the same effect in your garden. You have to be willing to experiment a bit and not be too concerned if you lose a plant or two to pests, disease, or improper soil nutrition. Observe, take notes, and learn from it!

Crop rotation is one of the best ways to prevent and control pests and disease in your vegetable garden. Crop rotation will help prevent problems and will build better soil, which will make for a healthier plant and harvest.

✳ *Smoothie Garden Solution*

The best way to attract beneficial insects to your garden is to provide them with plants that have nectar. Some useful plants are flowers and herbs such as nasturtiums, calendula, cosmos, basil, fennel, dill, caraway, and parsley. Planting them around your vegetable garden will help bring in beneficial insects.

Companion planting is another way to help keep the pests and disease out of your garden or at least under control. Intermix flowers and herbs among your vegetables to help ward off harmful insects and attract the beneficial ones.

Part III

Green Smoothies from the Garden

Chapter 15
Tasty Leaf Vegetables

A Spicy Assortment

From Your Garden: spinach, carrots, zucchini, celery

Ingredients
Recipe Yields: 3-4 cups

1 cup spinach

2 carrots, peeled

1 zucchini

1 celery

½ jalapeño, or to taste

½ orange, peeled

1 cup purified water

1. Combine spinach, carrots, zucchini, celery, jalapeño, orange, and ½ cup water in a blender and blend until thoroughly combined.
2. Add remaining water while blending until desired texture is achieved.

Antioxidant Assist

From Your Garden: spinach, broccoli

Ingredients
Recipe Yields: 3-4 cups

1 cup spinach

½ cup broccoli

1 banana

2 cups chamomile tea

1. Combine spinach, broccoli, banana, and 1 cup of tea in a blender and blend until thoroughly combined.
2. Add remaining 1 cup of tea as needed while blending until desired consistency is achieved.

Spice It Up!

From Your Garden: spinach, green onion, red bell pepper

Ingredients

Recipe Yields: 3-4 cups

1 cup spinach

1 green onion

½ red bell pepper, cored

½ cup mushrooms,
   stems intact

½ mango

2 tomatoes

2 cups purified water

PER 1 CUP SERVING
CALORIES: 119.2
FAT: 0.9g
PROTEIN: 3.5g
SODIUM: 29.1mg
FIBER: 3.9g
CARBOHYDRATES: 28.2g

1. Combine spinach, onion, red bell pepper, mushrooms, mango, tomatoes, and 1 cup of water in a blender and blend until thoroughly combined.
2. Add remaining 1 cup of water as needed while blending until desired consistency is achieved.

Veggies for Vitamins

From Your Garden: cucumber, celery, green onion, garlic

Ingredients

Recipe Yields: 3-4 cups

1 tomato

1 cucumber, peeled

1 celery stalk

1 green onion

1 garlic clove

½ mango

2 cups red mango tea

PER 1 CUP SERVING
CALORIES: 115.2
FAT: 0.8g
PROTEIN: 2g
SODIUM: 36.1mg
FIBER: 3.6g
CARBOHYDRATES: 28.1g

1. Combine tomato, cucumber, celery, onion, garlic, mango, and 1 cup of tea in a blender and blend until thoroughly combined.
2. Add remaining 1 cup of tea as needed while blending until desired consistency is achieved.

Veggie Delight

From Your Garden: romaine, zucchini, celery, cucumber, green onions, garlic

Ingredients
Recipe Yields: 4-6 cups

1 cup romaine lettuce

2 tomatoes

1 zucchini

2 celery stalks

1 cucumber, peeled

½ cup green onions

2 garlic cloves

1 orange, peeled

2 cups purified water

PER 1 CUP SERVING
CALORIES: 154.7
FAT: 1.3g
PROTEIN: 5.6g
SODIUM: 85mg
FIBER: 9g
CARBOHYDRATES: 34.6g

1. Combine romaine, tomatoes, zucchini, celery, cucumber, green onions, garlic, orange, and 1 cup water in a blender and blend until thoroughly combined.
2. Add remaining 1 cup of water as needed while blending until desired texture is achieved.

Colorful Collection

From Your Garden: romaine, broccoli, carrots

Ingredients
Recipe Yields: 3-4 cups

1 cup romaine lettuce

1 banana

1 cup broccoli

2 carrots, peeled

½ orange, peeled

2 cups chamomile tea

PER 1 CUP SERVING
CALORIES: 220.1
FAT: 1.3g
PROTEIN: 6g
SODIUM: 119.2mg
FIBER: 11.2g
CARBOHYDRATES: 52.8g

1. Combine romaine, banana, broccoli, carrots, orange, and 1 cup of tea in a blender and blend until thoroughly combined.
2. Add remaining 1 cup of tea as needed while blending until desired consistency is achieved.

Romaine to the Rescue!

From Your Garden: romaine, broccoli, carrots, garlic, orange pepper, basil

Ingredients
Recipe Yields: 3-4 cups

2 cups romaine lettuce
½ cup broccoli
2 carrots
1 garlic clove
½" ginger, peeled

1 orange pepper
1 orange, peeled
1 small tomato
¼ cup basil
2½ cups purified water

PER 1 CUP SERVING	
CALORIES: 150.8	
FAT: 1.4g	
PROTEIN: 6g	
SODIUM: 116.5mg	
FIBER: 11g	
CARBOHYDRATES: 32.3g	

1. Combine romaine, broccoli, carrots, garlic, ginger, pepper, orange, tomato, basil, and 1 ¼ cups of water in a blender and blend until thoroughly combined.
2. Add remaining 1 ¼ cups of water as needed while blending until desired consistency is achieved.

Savory Cancer Prevention

From Your Garden: cauliflower, lettuce, mint

Ingredients
Recipe Yields: 3-4 cups

½ cup cauliflower
½ cup grapes
½ cup almond milk
½ banana
1 cup lettuce

6 mint leaves
2 cups water

PER 1 CUP SERVING	
CALORIES: 104.4	
FAT: 0.6g	
PROTEIN: 2.6g	
SODIUM: 31.6mg	
FIBER: 3.6g	
CARBOHYDRATES: 25.4g	

1. Combine cauliflower, grapes, almond milk, banana, lettuce, mint, and 1 cup of water in a blender and blend until thoroughly combined.
2. Add remaining 1 cup of water as needed while blending until desired consistency is achieved.

Baby, Be Happy

From Your Garden: spinach, peas, carrots

Ingredients

Recipe Yields: 3-4 cups

1 cup spinach
1 cup sweet peas
3 carrots, peeled

1 banana
2 cups red raspberry tea

PER 1 CUP SERVING

CALORIES: 304.4

FAT: 1.5g

PROTEIN: 11.7g

SODIUM: 158.4mg

FIBER: 16.2g

CARBOHYDRATES: 66.5g

1. Combine spinach, peas, carrots, banana, and 1 cup of tea in a blender and blend until thoroughly combined.
2. Add remaining 1 cup of tea as needed while blending until desired consistency is achieved.

Savory Spinach

From Your Garden: spinach, red bell pepper, broccoli

Ingredients

Recipe Yields: 3-4 cups

1 cup spinach
½ red bell pepper, cored, ribs intact
½ cup broccoli spears

1 large pear
2 cups red raspberry tea

PER 1 CUP SERVING

CALORIES: 141.8

FAT: 0.7g

PROTEIN: 3.3g

SODIUM: 42.4mg

FIBER: 8.6g

CARBOHYDRATES: 34.7g

1. Combine spinach, red bell pepper, broccoli, pear, and 1 cup of tea in a blender and blend until thoroughly combined.
2. Add remaining 1 cup of tea as needed while blending until desired consistency is achieved.

Very Veggie

From Your Garden: spinach, celery, carrots, parsley

Ingredients

Recipe Yields: 3-4 cups

1 cup spinach

2 celery stalks

2 carrots, peeled

1 small sprig parsley

½ cup pineapple

1 cup purified water

PER 1 CUP SERVING
CALORIES: 103.3
FAT: 0.6g
PROTEIN: 2.9g
SODIUM: 159.7mg
FIBER: 6g
CARBOHYDRATES: 24.1g

1. Combine the spinach, celery, carrots, parsley, pineapple, and ½ cup water in a blender and blend until combined thoroughly.
2. If necessary, continue adding remaining water while blending until desired texture is achieved.

✳ *The Power of Parsley*

That green garnish that arrives as a decoration on the side of your plate is not given the attention it deserves! This green, leafy herb is rich in vitamins and minerals. In just 1 serving of this cleansing green, there are impressive amounts of vitamins K, C, and A, as well as iron and folate. By including just 2 tablespoons of parsley in your daily diet, you'll consume more than 153 percent of your needed vitamin K!

Imperative Iron

From Your Garden: kale, spinach

Ingredients

Recipe Yields: 3-4 cups

1 cup kale

1 cup spinach

½ orange, peeled

½ banana

½ cup almond milk

PER 1 CUP SERVING

CALORIES: 133.6

FAT: 1.1g

PROTEIN: 5.1g

SODIUM: 52.8mg

FIBER: 5.2g

CARBOHYDRATES: 30.9g

1. Combine kale, spinach, orange, banana, and almond milk in a blender and blend until thoroughly combined.

✳ *Why Pregnant Women Need More Iron*

Pregnant women require 27mg of iron per day (as opposed to 18mg when not pregnant). Because many women are iron-deficient prior to becoming pregnant, their needs are even higher, and the risks associated with iron deficiencies are more severe. Preterm delivery, low birth weight, and infant mortality are all risks of iron deficiencies in pregnancy. Ensure your body is provided with sufficient nonheme iron—the vitamin C from the broccoli will help improve the absorption of the nonheme iron.

Savory Slim-Down

From Your Garden: spinach, celery, green onion

Ingredients
Recipe Yields: 3-4 cups

1 cup spinach

1 stalk celery

1 tomato

1 green onion

1 pear

1 1/2 cups purified water

1. Combine spinach, celery, tomato, onion, pear, and 3/4 cup of the water in a blender and blend until thoroughly combined.
2. Add remaining 3/4 cup of water as needed while blending until desired consistency is achieved.

One Superb Herb

From Your Garden: iceberg lettuce, basil, cucumber

Ingredients

Recipe Yields: 3-4 cups

1 cup iceberg lettuce

½ cup basil

1 cucumber, peeled

½ cup pineapple

½ pear, cored, peeled,
   and chopped

½ cup purified water

PER 1 CUP SERVING
CALORIES: 104.9
FAT: 0.4g
PROTEIN: 1.8g
SODIUM: 9.4mg
FIBER: 5g
CARBOHYDRATES: 26.9g

1. Combine the iceberg lettuce, basil, cucumber, pineapple, pear, and half of the water in a blender and blend until combined thoroughly.
2. If needed, continue adding remaining water while blending until desired texture is achieved.

✳ *Basil and Vitamin K*

Although the greens blended into green smoothies offer vitamin K, the added benefit of using basil can be quite astounding. While many greens servings may offer a healthy helping of Vitamin K, just 2 teaspoons (or 3 grams) of basil can account for 60 percent of your RDA of vitamin K. You might fulfill, or even surpass, your recommended amount of vitamin K by just mixing the greens and basil in one smoothie!

Chapter 16
Delicious Brassicas and Roots

Beet Booster

From Your Garden: beet greens, beets

Ingredients

Recipe Yields: 3-4 cups

1 cup beet greens

1 small beet

1 banana, peeled

2 cups purified water

PER 1 CUP SERVING

CALORIES: 148.6

FAT: 0.6g

PROTEIN: 3.4g

SODIUM: 151mg

FIBER: 6.8g

CARBOHYDRATES: 36.4g

1. Combine beet greens, beet, banana, and 1 cup of water in a blender and blend until thoroughly combined.
2. Add remaining cup of water while blending until desired texture is achieved.

A Sweet Beet to Step To

From Your Garden: radicchio, beets

Ingredients

Recipe Yields: 2-3 cups

1 cup radicchio
1 small beet
10 medium strawberries
1 cup Greek-style yogurt

PER 1 CUP SERVING
CALORIES: 78.8
FAT: 0.1g
PROTEIN: 5.4g
SODIUM: 75mg
FIBER: 0.5g
CARBOHYDRATES: 13.6g

1. Combine the radicchio, beet, strawberries, and ½ cup Greek-style yogurt in a blender and blend to combine thoroughly.
2. While blending, add remaining ½ cup yogurt until desired texture is achieved.

✳ *Reddening Effects of Beets*

If you are new to consuming beets, you should know that you will see some reddening in the smoothie, and more than you would expect. Although not a cause for concern, following beet consumption, urine may turn a slightly reddish or light-purple color, most often found in people with deficient or excess amounts of iron.

A Sweet Beet Treat

From Your Garden: beet greens, beets

Ingredients

Recipe Yields: 3-4 cups

1 cup beet greens

1 small beet

5 large strawberries

1 banana, peeled

1 cup almond milk

½ cup ice cubes
  (optional)

PER 1 CUP SERVING
CALORIES: 237.4
FAT: 3.3g
PROTEIN: 5g
SODIUM: 301.9mg
FIBER: 9.6g
CARBOHYDRATES: 51.3g

1. Combine beet greens, beet, strawberries, banana, and ½ cup almond milk in a blender and blend until thoroughly combined.
2. Add remaining almond milk and ice while blending until desired texture is achieved.

✳ *Beet Greens*

While the actual beets are what have the reputation for being sweet, nutritious, delicious little veggies, the greens of the beet are also edible and highly nutritious. Packed with calcium, potassium, and vitamins A and C, the leaves of these powerful, deep-purple veggies are a healthy addition to any diet.

Carrot Top of the Morning to You

From Your Garden: romaine, carrots

Ingredients

Recipe Yields: 4 cups

2 cups romaine lettuce

3 carrots, peeled and cut
   into sticks

1 apple, peeled, cored,
   and chopped

1 cup purified water

PER 1 CUP SERVING
CALORIES: 42
FAT: 0g
PROTEIN: 1g
SODIUM: 35mg
FIBER: 2g
CARBOHYDRATES: 10g

1. Combine romaine, carrots, and apple in a blender.
2. Add water slowly while blending until desired texture is achieved.

❋ *Carrots Can Save the Day!*

With the ability to protect your body from cancer, heart attacks, premature aging, and poor vision, this vegetable is a must-have in your daily diet. Its rich orange color is the telltale sign that it is rich in beta carotene (vitamin A), but it's also packed with B vitamins, biotin, vitamin K, and potassium. Talk about a multitasker!

Sweet Veggie Surprise

From Your Garden: spinach, carrots, beet, red bell pepper

Ingredients

Recipe Yields: 3-4 cups

1 cup spinach
1 tomato
4 carrots, peeled
½ mango
1 beet
½ red bell pepper, cored with ribs intact
2 ½ cups purified water

PER 1 CUP SERVING
CALORIES: 186.1
FAT: 1.3g
PROTEIN: 4.9g
SODIUM: 198.4mg
FIBER: 10.8g
CARBOHYDRATES: 42.8g

1. Combine spinach, tomato, carrots, mango, beet, red bell pepper, and 1 ¼ cups of water in a blender and blend until thoroughly combined.
2. Add remaining 1 ¼ cups of the water as needed while blending until desired consistency is achieved.

Carrot Cleanser

From Your Garden: spinach, carrots

Ingredients

Recipe Yields: 3–4 cups

1 cup spinach
4 carrots, peeled and tops removed
1 lemon, peeled
2 cups purified water

PER 1 CUP SERVING
CALORIES: 31
FAT: 0g
PROTEIN: 1g
SODIUM: 51mg
FIBER: 2g
CARBOHYDRATES: 7g

1. Combine spinach, carrots, lemon, and 1 cup of water in a blender and blend until thoroughly combined.
2. Add remaining 1 cup of water while blending as needed until desired texture is achieved.

Carrots as Superfoods

Harnessing the powerful vitamins and minerals contained in carrots while you're on a detoxifying cleanse can help in many ways. The beta carotene that gives carrots their vibrant color is not only important for eye health, but is also a strong cancer-fighting antioxidant that protects cells against harmful free radicals and promotes optimal cell functioning. Carrots also lower the risk of heart disease, cancers, and type 2 diabetes, and provide sound nutrition for pregnancy and night vision.

Apple Carrot

From Your Garden: watercress, carrots, celery, garlic

Ingredients

Recipe Yields: 3-4 cups

1 cup watercress

1 apple, cored, peeled, and chopped

3 carrots, peeled

1 celery stalk

1 garlic clove

2 cups purified water

PER 1 CUP SERVING

CALORIES: 166.9

FAT: 0.8g

PROTEIN: 3.4g

SODIUM: 172.7mg

FIBER: 8.1g

CARBOHYDRATES: 40.7g

1. Combine watercress, apple, carrots, celery, garlic, and 1 cup water in a blender and blend until thoroughly combined.
2. Add remaining 1 cup of water as needed while blending until desired consistency is achieved.

Colorful Cleansing Combo

From Your Garden: watercress, carrots, cucumber

Ingredients

Recipe Yields: 3-4 cups

1 cup watercress

3 carrots, peeled

1 cucumber

½ cup pineapple

2 cups purified water

PER 1 CUP SERVING

CALORIES: 144.1

FAT: 0.9g

PROTEIN: 4.1g

SODIUM: 145.1mg

FIBER: 7.9g

CARBOHYDRATES: 33.1g

1. Combine watercress, carrots, cucumber, pineapple, and 1 cup of water in a blender and blend until thoroughly combined.
2. Add remaining 1 cup of water while blending as needed until desired texture is achieved.

✳ *Taste the Rainbow for Optimal Health*

It may be difficult to figure out which food group is best for your body and promoting its ideal functioning. The answer is . . . all of them! The easiest route to achieving optimum health is to taste the rainbow: Eat a variety of different foods with vibrant colors. By consuming a variety of fruits and vegetables with color, you can ensure your body is receiving abundant vitamins and nutrients. With variety comes the added benefit of never becoming tired of the same old fruit or veggie.

Blazing Broccoli

From Your Garden: spinach, broccoli, carrot

Ingredients
Recipe Yields: 3-4 cups

1 cup spinach
1 cup broccoli
1 carrot, peeled

1 banana
½ lime, peeled
2 cups purified water

PER 1 CUP SERVING
CALORIES: 177.9
FAT: 1.1g
PROTEIN: 5.5g
SODIUM: 97.7mg
FIBER: 8.7g
CARBOHYDRATES: 43.5g

1. Combine spinach, broccoli, carrot, banana, lime, and 1 cup of purified water in a blender and blend until thoroughly combined.
2. Add remaining 1 cup water while blending until desired texture is achieved.

Broccoli Blastoff

From Your Garden: kale, broccoli, celery, garlic

Ingredients
Recipe Yields: 3-4 cups

2 kale leaves
1 cup broccoli
1 banana
2 celery stalks
½ orange, peeled

1-2 garlic cloves,
    depending on size
2 cups purified water

PER 1 CUP SERVING
CALORIES: 172.4
FAT: 1.1g
PROTEIN: 5.6g
SODIUM: 102.6mg
FIBER: 7.5g
CARBOHYDRATES: 40.5g

1. Combine kale, broccoli, banana, celery, orange, garlic, and 1 cup of water in a blender and blend until thoroughly combined.
2. Add remaining 1 cup of water as needed while blending until desired consistency is achieved.

The Spicy Savior

From Your Garden: watercress, broccoli, carrots

Ingredients
Recipe Yields: 3-4 cups

1 cup watercress
1 cup broccoli spears
3 carrots, peeled
1/2" ginger, peeled

1 pear, cored, peeled, and chopped
2 cups purified water

PER 1 CUP SERVING
CALORIES: 212.8
FAT: 1.1g
PROTEIN: 5.7g
SODIUM: 172.3mg
FIBER: 13.2g
CARBOHYDRATES: 51.5g

1. Combine watercress, broccoli, carrots, ginger, pear, and 1 cup of water in a blender and blend until thoroughly combined.
2. Add remaining 1 cup of water while blending as needed until desired texture is achieved.

Parsley Pride

From Your Garden: spinach, zucchini, parsley

Ingredients
Recipe Yields: 3-4 cups

1 cup spinach
1 zucchini, skin intact
1/4 cup parsley

1/2 cup pineapple
2 cups purified water

PER 1 CUP SERVING
CALORIES: 55.9
FAT: 0.4g
PROTEIN: 2g
SODIUM: 33.3mg
FIBER: 2.4g
CARBOHYDRATES: 13.2g

1. Combine the spinach, zucchini, parsley, pineapple, and 1 cup of water in a blender and blend until thoroughly combined.
2. Add remaining 1 cup of water while blending as needed until desired texture is achieved.

Garlic and Onions Keep the Doctor Away

From Your Garden: watercress, celery, green onion, zucchini, garlic

Ingredients

Recipe Yields: 3-4 cups

1 cup watercress	1 tomato
1 celery stalk	½ mango
1 green onion	2 cups purified water
1 zucchini	
1 garlic clove	

PER 1 CUP SERVING

CALORIES: 132.1

FAT: 1g

PROTEIN: 3.6g

SODIUM: 53.4mg

FIBER: 4.6g

CARBOHYDRATES: 31.2g

1. Combine watercress, celery, onion, zucchini, garlic, tomato, mango, and 1 cup of water in a blender and blend until thoroughly combined.
2. Add remaining 1 cup of water as needed while blending until desired consistency is achieved.

The Zesty Zoomer

From Your Garden: red bell pepper, cilantro, zucchini

Ingredients

Recipe Yields: 3-4 cups

1 red bell pepper, cored	½ zucchini
2 tablespoons cilantro	2 cups purified water
½ cup raspberries	
5 medium strawberries	

PER 1 CUP SERVING

CALORIES: 89.2

FAT: 1g

PROTEIN: 2.5g

SODIUM: 6.1mg

FIBER: 7.8g

CARBOHYDRATES: 19.3g

1. Combine pepper, cilantro, raspberries, strawberries, zucchini, and 1 cup water in a blender and blend until thoroughly combined.
2. Add remaining 1 cup water as needed while blending until desired texture is achieved.

Chapter 17
Peppy Peppers, Herbs, and More

Green Gazpacho

From Your Garden: watercress, cucumber, celery, green bell pepper, garlic, basil

Ingredients

Recipe Yields: 3-4 cups

1 cup watercress

2 tomatoes

1 cucumber, peeled

1 celery stalk

½ red onion

½ green bell pepper

3 garlic cloves

1 small jalapeño (optional)

3 tablespoons red
   wine vinegar

2 tablespoons basil
   leaves, chopped

1 cup purified water,
   if needed

PER 1 CUP SERVING
CALORIES: 34
FAT: 0g
PROTEIN: 2g
SODIUM: 18mg
FIBER: 2g
CARBOHYDRATES: 7g

1. Combine watercress, tomatoes, cucumber, celery, onion, pepper, garlic, jalapeño, vinegar, and basil in a blender and blend until thoroughly combined.
2. If needed, slowly add purified water while blending until desired texture is achieved.

✳ *A Vegetable Fiesta in Your Blender*

This popular vegetable soup is served cold, and is absolutely packed with a wide variety of vegetables! Between the watercress, cucumber, celery, tomatoes, onion, peppers, and herbs, there aren't many vitamins and minerals left out of this smoothie. The green color, fresh taste, and zing that can only come from a combination of veggies like these are delivered in this powerfully packed smoothie.

Powerful Pepper Trio

From Your Garden: red bell pepper, green bell pepper, yellow bell pepper, garlic

Ingredients
Recipe Yields: 3-4 cups

1 banana

1 red bell pepper, cored

1 green bell pepper,
    cored

1 yellow bell pepper,
    cored

1 garlic clove

2 cups purified water

PER 1 CUP SERVING
CALORIES: 220.2
FAT: 1.5g
PROTEIN: 5g
SODIUM: 16mg
FIBER: 10.6g
CARBOHYDRATES: 49.5g

1. Combine banana, peppers, garlic, and 1 cup of water in a blender and blend until thoroughly combined.
2. Add remaining 1 cup water while blending until desired texture is achieved.

A Peppery Way to Promote Health

From Your Garden: celery, red bell pepper, garlic

Ingredients
Recipe Yields: 3-4 cups

1 tomato

2 celery stalks

½ red bell pepper, cored
    with ribs intact

10 medium strawberries

1 garlic clove

1 ½ cups water

PER 1 CUP SERVING
CALORIES: 86.5
FAT: 0.8g
PROTEIN: 2.7g
SODIUM: 71.2mg
FIBER: 6g
CARBOHYDRATES: 18.6g

1. Combine tomato, celery, red bell pepper, strawberries, garlic, and ³/₄ cup of the water in a blender and blend until thoroughly combined.
2. Add remaining ³/₄ cup of the water as needed while blending until desired consistency is achieved.

Red Pepper Relief

From Your Garden: romaine, red bell pepper, celery

Ingredients
Recipe Yields: 3-4 cups

1 cup romaine lettuce

1 red bell pepper, top and seeds removed, ribs intact

2 celery stalks, leaves intact

½ lemon, peeled

1 pear, cored, peeled, and chopped

1 ½ cups chamomile tea

PER 1 CUP SERVING
CALORIES: 167.6
FAT: 1g
PROTEIN: 3.3g
SODIUM: 74.9mg
FIBER: 11.1g
CARBOHYDRATES: 40.9g

1. Combine romaine, red bell pepper, celery, lemon, pear, and ¾ cup of tea in a blender and blend until thoroughly combined.
2. Add remaining ¾ cup of tea as needed while blending until desired consistency is achieved.

Zap Pounds with Zippy Zucchini

From Your Garden: kale, zucchini, red bell pepper, green onion, garlic

Ingredients
Recipe Yields: 3-4 cups

2 kale leaves

1 zucchini, peeled

1 orange, peeled

½ red bell pepper

1 green onion

2 garlic cloves

2 cups purified water

PER 1 CUP SERVING
CALORIES: 62.4
FAT: 0.7g
PROTEIN: 3g
SODIUM: 18.3mg
FIBER: 3g
CARBOHYDRATES: 12.8g

1. Combine kale, zucchini, orange, red bell pepper, onion, garlic, and 1 cup water in a blender and blend until thoroughly combined.
2. Add remaining 1 cup of water as needed while blending until desired consistency is achieved.

Peas for a Perfect Pregnancy

From Your Garden: peas, celery, cucumber

Ingredients

Recipe Yields: 3-4 cups

½ cup pineapple
1 cup sweet peas
2 celery stalks
1 cucumber, peeled

½ banana
1 cup red raspberry
   tea

PER 1 CUP SERVING

CALORIES: 248.1

FAT: 1.3g

PROTEIN: 10.7g

SODIUM: 76.7mg

FIBER: 12.8g

CARBOHYDRATES: 52g

1. Combine pineapple, sweet peas, celery, cucumber, banana, and ½ cup tea in a blender and blend until thoroughly combined.
2. Add remaining ½-cup of tea as needed while blending until desired consistency is achieved.

Peas to the World!

From Your Garden: spinach, carrots, celery, peas

Ingredients

Recipe Yields: 3-4 cups

1 cup spinach
2 carrots, peeled
3 celery stalks, leaves
   intact
¾ cup petite sweet peas

1 pear, cored, peeled,
   and chopped
2 cups chamomile tea

PER 1 CUP SERVING

CALORIES: 265.7

FAT: 1.3g

PROTEIN: 9.4g

SODIUM: 211.1mg

FIBER: 17.1g

CARBOHYDRATES: 59.2g

1. Combine spinach, carrots, celery, peas, pear, and 1 cup of tea in a blender and blend until thoroughly combined.
2. Add remaining 1 cup of tea as needed while blending until desired consistency is achieved.

Peas, Please!

From Your Garden: spinach, peas, carrots

Ingredients

Recipe Yields: 3–4 cups

1 cup spinach

1 cup sweet peas

2 carrots, peeled

1 apple, cored, peeled,
 and chopped

1 cup green tea

1 cup ice

PER 1 CUP SERVING
CALORIES: 60
FAT: 0g
PROTEIN: 2g
SODIUM: 64mg
FIBER: 3g
CARBOHYDRATES: 13g

1. Combine spinach, peas, carrots, apple, and tea in a blender and blend until thoroughly combined.
2. Add ice as needed while blending until desired consistency is achieved.

❋ *The Lonely Sweet Pea*

Very rarely do kids get heaping helpings of peas on a regular basis. Providing more than 50 percent of the recommended daily amount of vitamin K and packed with vitamin Bs, C, folate, iron, zinc, manganese, and protein, peas are a great choice for a regular addition to any child's diet. Promoting brain health, bone strength, heart health, and disease-fighting protection, these sweet green morsels are worth their weight in health!

"Pea" Is for Prevention

From Your Garden: watercress, cucumbers, peas

Ingredients

Recipe Yields: 3-4 cups

1 cup watercress

2 cucumbers, peeled

1 cup petite sweet
   green peas

1 banana

2 cups purified water

PER 1 CUP SERVING	
CALORIES: 226.5	
FAT: 1g	
PROTEIN: 9.9g	
SODIUM: 22.4mg	
FIBER: 10.6g	
CARBOHYDRATES: 48.4g	

1. Combine watercress, cucumbers, peas, banana, and 1 cup of water in a blender and blend until thoroughly combined.
2. Add remaining 1 cup of water as needed while blending until desired consistency is achieved.

✳ *The Power of a Pea*

Adding just 1 cup of this sweet veggie to your daily diet will provide over 50 percent of your daily recommended intake of vitamin K, along with vitamins B and C, manganese, folate, fiber, and protein. This results in stronger bones; heightened disease prevention; efficient metabolism of carbohydrates, fats, and proteins; improved cardiac health; and more energy.

Calming Cucumber

From Your Garden: romaine, cucumbers, mint

Ingredients

Recipe Yields: 3-4 cups

1 cup romaine lettuce

2 cucumbers, peeled

¼ cup mint, chopped

1 cup watermelon

1 cup purified water

PER 1 CUP SERVING
CALORIES: 93.5
FAT: 0.9g
PROTEIN: 3.6g
SODIUM: 22.9mg
FIBER: 6.1g
CARBOHYDRATES: 21.5g

1. Combine romaine, cucumbers, mint, watermelon, and ½ cup water in a blender and combine thoroughly.
2. Add remaining water while blending until desired texture is achieved.

✳ *Cucumbers Aren't Just Water*

Even though a cucumber is mostly water (and fiber), it is far more than a tasty, hydrating, and filling snack option. These green veggies are a great addition to a diet in need of moisture and clarity . . . for the skin! A clear complexion is an aesthetic benefit of consuming cucumbers. By consuming 1 serving of cucumbers per day, you'll not only fulfill a full serving of veggies and stave off hunger, you'll have clear, hydrated skin!

Cool Cucumber Melon

From Your Garden: romaine, mint, cucumbers

Ingredients

Recipe Yields: 3-4 cups

1 cup romaine lettuce
1 sprig mint leaves
3 cucumbers, peeled

½ honeydew melon,
    peeled, seeds removed
½ cup kefir

PER 1 CUP SERVING
CALORIES: 86
FAT: 1g
PROTEIN: 3g
SODIUM: 43mg
FIBER: 3g
CARBOHYDRATES: 17g

1. In a blender, combine romaine and mint leaves followed by the cucumbers, melon, and half of the kefir and blend until thoroughly combined.
2. Add remaining half of kefir while blending until desired texture is achieved.

✳ *Cucumbers and Skin*

If you're exfoliating, hydrating, and moisturizing your skin but still feel like you're not reaching that desired clarity and glow, try working on your complexion from the inside. Packed with the powerful combination of vitamin A and silica, cucumbers can help repair connective tissue and skin. So, instead of buying that new and improved face cream, include a couple of servings of cucumbers for that healthy skin you desire!

Green Machine

From Your Garden: celery, cucumber, spinach, cilantro

Ingredients
Recipe Yields: 3-4 cups

1 stalk celery

½ cucumber

1 green apple, cored,
    peeled, and chopped

1 cup spinach

¼ cup cilantro

lime juice from ½ lime

1 cup water

PER 1 CUP SERVING:

CALORIES: 131

FAT: 0.7g

PROTEIN: 2.7g

SODIUM: 62.4mg

FIBER: 6.5g

CARBOHYDRATES: 33g

1. In a blender combine the celery, cucumber, apple, spinach, cilantro, lime juice, and ½ cup of water and blend until thoroughly combined.
2. Add remaining ½ cup of water while blending until desired texture is achieved.

Standard U.S./Metric Measurement Conversions

VOLUME CONVERSIONS

U.S. Volume Measure	Metric Equivalent
⅛ teaspoon	0.5 milliliter
¼ teaspoon	1 milliliter
½ teaspoon	2 milliliters
1 teaspoon	5 milliliters
½ tablespoon	7 milliliters
1 tablespoon (3 teaspoons)	15 milliliters
2 tablespoons (1 fluid ounce)	30 milliliters
¼ cup (4 tablespoons)	60 milliliters
⅓ cup	90 milliliters
½ cup (4 fluid ounces)	125 milliliters
⅔ cup	160 milliliters
¾ cup (6 fluid ounces)	180 milliliters
1 cup (16 tablespoons)	250 milliliters
1 pint (2 cups)	500 milliliters
1 quart (4 cups)	1 liter (about)

WEIGHT CONVERSIONS

U.S. Weight Measure	Metric Equivalent
½ ounce	15 grams
1 ounce	30 grams
2 ounces	60 grams
3 ounces	85 grams
¼ pound (4 ounces)	115 grams
½ pound (8 ounces)	225 grams
¾ pound (12 ounces)	340 grams
1 pound (16 ounces)	454 grams

OVEN TEMPERATURE CONVERSIONS

Degrees Fahrenheit	Degrees Celsius
200 degrees F	95 degrees C
250 degrees F	120 degrees C
275 degrees F	135 degrees C
300 degrees F	150 degrees C
325 degrees F	160 degrees C
350 degrees F	180 degrees C
375 degrees F	190 degrees C
400 degrees F	205 degrees C
425 degrees F	220 degrees C
450 degrees F	230 degrees C

BAKING PAN SIZES

U.S.	Metric
8 × 1½ inch round baking pan	20 × 4 cm cake tin
9 × 1½ inch round baking pan	23 × 3.5 cm cake tin
11 × 7 × 1½ inch baking pan	28 × 18 × 4 cm baking tin
13 × 9 × 2 inch baking pan	30 × 20 × 5 cm baking tin
2 quart rectangular baking dish	30 × 20 × 3 cm baking tin
15 × 10 × 2 inch baking pan	30 × 25 × 2 cm baking tin (Swiss roll tin)
9 inch pie plate	22 × 4 or 23 × 4 cm pie plate
7 or 8 inch springform pan	18 or 20 cm springform or loose bottom cake tin
9 × 5 × 3 inch loaf pan	23 × 13 × 7 cm or 2 lb narrow loaf or pâté tin
1½ quart casserole	1.5 liter casserole
2 quart casserole	2 liter casserole

Appendix A
Web and Book Resources

The author acknowledges the following websites and books for the inspiration they gave during the research and writing of this book. If you want more information, check out these resources on small-space gardening.

Web Resources

Your Vegetable Gardening Helper

This site has some great "how-to" steps and some garden design books to help you to have a fabulous vegetable garden.

www.your-vegetable-gardening-helper.com

Kitchen Gardeners International

A site teaching the importance of growing your own food in order to live a healthier lifestyle, and have a healthier community and planet.

www.kgi.org

Grow Your Own Groceries

This site promotes and gives instructions on growing food in your backyard.

www.growyourowngroceries.org

Straw Bale Gardens

A site introducing straw-bale gardening.

www.strawbalegardens.com

The Rooftop Garden Project

Learn about rooftop gardening.

www.insideurbangreen.org/rooftop-garden-project---montreal/

Fine Gardening

An online magazine with a variety of gardening topics.
www.finegardening.com

Mother Earth News

Online magazine with articles promoting self-sustainability, organic gardening, and living off the land.
www.motherearthnews.com

Urban Garden Casual

This site promotes and gives information on setting up urban gardens.
www.urbangardencasual.com

About.com: Organic Gardening

A site with a variety of topics promoting organic gardening.
www.organicgardening.about.com

No Dig Vegetable Garden

This site promotes and teaches the no dig gardening method.
www.no-dig-vegetablegarden.com

Food4Wealth

Videos giving tips and instructions on low-cost garden tips for growing organic vegetables.
www.homeorganicgarden.net

Book Resources

Catherine Abbott. *The Everything® Grow Your Own Vegetables Book*. (Massachusetts: F+W Media, Inc., 2010).

Catherine Abbott. *The Everything® Root Cellaring Book*. (Massachusetts: F+W Media, Inc., 2011).

Catherine Abbott. *Vegetable Garden Plans for Row Gardening*. (Canada: Self-published, 2008).

Catherine Abbott. *Vegetable Garden Plans for Square Foot Gardens*. (Canada: Self-published, 2008).

Catherine Abbott. *Vegetable Garden Plans for Your Raised Beds*. (Canada: Self-published, 2008).

Mel Bartholomew. *Square Foot Gardening*. (New York: St. Martin's Press, 1981).

Graham Bell. *The Permaculture Garden*. (Hampshire, UK: Permanent Publications, 2004).

Jennifer Bennett. *The Harrowsmith Book of Fruit Trees*. (Canada: Camden House Publishing, 1991).

Sally Jean Cunningham. *Great Garden Companions*. (Emmaus, PA: Rodale Press Inc., 1998).

Eugene Davenport. *Domesticated Animals and Plants*. (Boston and New York: Gin and Company, 1910).

Nigel Dunnett and Noel Kingsbury. *Planting Green Roofs and Living Walls*. (Portland, OR: Timber Press Inc., 2008).

Bob Flowerdew. *The No-Work Garden*. (Canada: Whitecap Books, 2002).

Marjorie Harris. *Pocket Gardening: A Guide to Gardening in Impossible Places*. (Canada: HarperCollins Canada, Ltd., 1998).

D. G. Hessayon. *The Container Expert*. (London: Transworld Publishers Ltd., 1995).

Erin Hynes. *Rodale's Weekend Gardener*. (Emmaus, PA: Rodale Press Inc., 1998).

Patricia Lanza. *Lasagna Gardening with Herbs*. (Emmaus, PA: Rodale Press, Inc., 2004).

Patricia Lanza. *Lasagna Gardening for Small Spaces*. (Emmaus, PA: Rodale Press, Inc., 2002).

Clare Matthews. *Great Gardens for Kids*. (London: Octopus Publishing Group Ltd., 2002).

Duane Newcomb and Karen Newcomb. *The Postage Stamp Garden*. (Massachusetts: Adams Media Corporation, 1999).

Sue Phillips. *A Creative Step-By-Step Guide to Urban Gardens*. (Canada: Whitecap Books, 1995).

Sue Phillips and Neil Sutherland. *A Creative Step-By-Step Guide to Patio Gardening*. (Canada: Whitecap Books, 1994).

Ruth Stout. *Gardening Without Work*. (New York: The Devin-Adair Company, 1963).

Ruth Stout. *How to Have a Green Thumb Without an Aching Back: A New Method of Mulch Gardening*. (New York: Exposition Press, 1955).

Sunset Books. *Plant Containers You Can Make*. (Menlo Park: Lane Publishing Co., 1976).

Appendix B
Glossary

ANNUAL

A plant that completes its growing cycle in one season. It grows and does not come back the following season.

ARBOR

A small-scale garden shelter usually made of wood or lattice with plants climbing all over it.

BIENNIAL

A plant that requires two growing seasons to complete its life cycle. Leaves and stems grow the first season with the flowers and seeds forming the second year.

COMPANION PLANTING

Plants that have an influence on each other, either beneficial or harmful.

COMPOST HEAP

A compost heap is made up of vegetable scraps and plant discards. When you pile all of this together it will begin to rot over time, making a great fertilizer to put back into your garden.

COOL CROPS

Vegetables that grow and produce better in cooler weather, such as peas, lettuce, spinach, and cabbage.

CROP ROTATION

Growing annual vegetable plants in a different location in the garden each year. This helps to control insects, improves soil fertility, and helps to prevent soil erosion.

CULTIVATE

To prepare soil for planting by plowing, digging, and fertilizing or it can mean you cultivate the earth by digging around the root of a plant.

DRAINAGE

The running off of water gradually from the earth where your plants are growing. Good drainage ensures your plants get the moisture they need but the moisture does not collect, leaving the roots waterlogged.

DWARF ROOTSTOCK

A rootstock of diminished vigor, which produces a smaller mature plant or tree.

ESPALIER

A lattice made of wood or wire on which to train fruit trees by selecting lateral branches to grow horizontally on each side of a main stem.

FERTILIZER

Extra nourishment for your plants. Air, water, and nutrients are essential for plant growth. Sometimes the soil does not have enough nutrients so additional nourishment needs to be added, usually in the form or organic matter or manmade fertilizer.

FERTILIZER TEA

A mix of organic materials intended to bolster the health of growing vegetable plants.

GAZEBO

A garden pavilion, usually designed to offer a view, shelter, or place to sit.

GERMINATE

To begin to grow or sprout a plant from a seed.

GREEN MANURE

Crops such as legumes or grasses grown in the fall to be dug under in the spring. Used to increase the organic matter in garden soil, which will improve the soil structure.

HUMUS

Partially or totally decayed vegetable matter, which is food for plants and helps soil retain moisture.

INTERPLANTING

Planting to get maximum production from your garden or container. This is done by planting vegetables that mature early in the season alongside plants that mature later in the season.

LEGGY

Describes weak-stemmed and spindly vegetable seedlings. This is usually caused by too much heat, too much shade, crowding, or over-fertilization.

LIME

A compound containing calcium and magnesium. It is applied to garden soil to reduce acidity.

LOAM

Soil that consists of a mixture of sand, silt, and clay. It is an ideal garden soil for growing vegetable plants.

MANURE

Animal waste used as a soil amendment and fertilizer. You want to use aged manures in order not to harm the plants.

MICROCLIMATE

A climate particular to a specific situation, which differs from the overall climate of an area—against a wall or hedge as an example.

MICROORGANISM

A microscopic animal or plant that may cause disease or may have a beneficial effect when a plant is decomposing.

MULCH

A protective covering of rotted organic matter such as straw, leaves, peat moss, wood chips, and grass clippings used to keep the weeds from growing as well as protecting plant roots.

NEMATODES

A variety of parasitic worm that lives in the soil.

ORGANIC MATTER

A portion of the soil that is a result of decomposition of plant and animal residue. It helps maintain good soil structure and promotes microorganisms in the soil.

PEAT MOSS

A kind of moss that grows in very wet places. It is gathered, processed, and then sold to be used in mulching, as plant food, or mixed into soil.

PERENNIAL
A plant that lives for more than two years.

PERGOLA
A walk of pillars and cross members with plants trained to grow up over it.

pH
A chemical symbol used to identify the level of acidity and alkalinity in soil. The scale ranges from 0 to 14, with 7.0 being neutral. Readings of less than 7.0 indicate acidic soil and readings of above 7.0 indicate alkaline soil.

PLANT RESIDUE
Plant parts such as leaves, stem, and roots that remain after a vegetable has been harvested. These parts can be used to make compost.

POTAGER
A French term for a small vegetable garden.

PROPAGATE
To cause plants to increase, spread, and multiply. Bees, insects, and the wind carry pollen from flower to flower to fertilize plants.

PRUNE
To cut off branches or leaves to make room for healthy new growth on trees and plants.

RIPE
The stage of maturity at which the fruit or vegetable is ready to be harvested and eaten.

ROOTSTOCK
A root or plant on which can be grafted certain species that are difficult to propagate from their own roots.

SEEDLING
A very young vegetable plant.

SELF-FERTILE
Describes a plant whose ovule is fertilized by its own pollen and grows into viable seed.

SELF-SEEDING
Describes a plant, usually an annual, that will regenerate from year to year by dispersing its seeds around an area.

SELF-STERILE
Describes a plant whose ovules require pollen from another plant (the pollinator) in order to grow viable seed.

SHORT-SEASON VEGETABLE
These are vegetables that are ready for harvesting one or two months following planting.

SILT
Soil particles that are between the size of sand and clay.

SLOW-RELEASE FERTILIZER
A substance that releases the essential nutrients for the growth of a plant over a long period of time.

SOIL

This is the upper layer of the earth's surface. It is composed of organic matter, minerals, and microorganisms, all making it capable of supporting plant life.

SOW

To scatter seed over the ground you have prepared for planting.

STAKE

To tie plants to a sturdy stick for support to grow upright.

TENDER

Describes plants likely to be damaged by low temperatures.

THIN OUT

As plants grow you must take some of them out of the ground to leave room for others to have enough space to grow bigger.

TRANSPLANT

To move young plants from one place to another. You take a plant from a pot and put it into the ground.

TYING IN

The action of securing climbers to a support, a wall, a trellis, or a stake.

VARIETY

Closely related vegetable plants forming a subdivision of a species that have similar characteristics.

Index

Includes Small-Space Gardening Techniques

GREEN SMOOTHIES STRAIGHT FROM YOUR GARDEN

Smoothies blended with fresh, crisp greens and natural fruit juices will increase your daily vegetable intake, boost your energy, and improve your overall well-being—and they don't have to cost a fortune! *The Green Smoothie Garden* teaches you how to make the healthiest green smoothies without breaking the bank. Featuring simple instructions and valuable gardening tips, this book shows you how to grow the vegetables in your favorite smoothies and incorporate them into a variety of delicious recipes. From kale to spinach to collards, the nutrient-rich greens featured in these tasty smoothies can be produced in any gardening space, so you'll be able to reap the benefits of a homegrown green smoothie no matter where you live.

The Green Smoothie Garden gives you the advice and tools you need to make the most nutritious drinks right at home and at a fraction of the cost!

Tracy Russell is the founder of the popular green smoothie website IncredibleSmoothies.com. After her own success with smoothies, she and her husband created a sustainable weight-loss program, which she shares with her fans through an e-course.

Catherine Abbott grew vegetables in her suburban backyard until 2000, when she started a small-scale vegetable farm. She now grows fabulous vegetables that she sells in her local community, as well as teaches gardening classes and runs the popular website *www.your-vegetable-gardening-helper.com*.

Cover design by Frank Rivera
Cover images © 123rf.com/ Maryana Teslenko

$16.99 (CAN $18.99)   Gardening
ISBN-13: 978-1-4405-6837-4
ISBN-10: 1-4405-6837-5

EAN
9 781440 568374

5 1699

UPC   0 45079 56837 2

Aadamsmedia
www.adamsmedia.com